GOING ON MY OWN

21st CENTURY LEGAL TALES:

A Memoir of Life As an International Lawyer

By Robert Layton

FIRST EDITION

ISBN-13: 978-1482014518

ISBN-10: 1482014513

Cover photo by Bruce Rolff, licensed via 123RF.com

I, a stranger and afraid,
In a world I never made.
"Last Poems" by A. E. Housman

TABLE OF CONTENTS

This book is dedicated
to my daughters,
Elisabeth and Julie.

Foreword

This memoir has been formed in early part by notes taken by me while waiting in airports between connecting flights, or in strange hotels, while on legal assignments in foreign countries. It occurred to me that I should make notes of any unusual occurrences in order that I not forget them, and did so in a black-and-white-spotted Mead Composition Book of the kind used in my secondary school days for penmanship exercises and school homework. It has stood me in good stead over the years and my skimpy notes have been sufficient for me to now recall more fully, some of the events, which I can now describe in some detail. It has been a pretty interesting ride. Now hold on!

Reflecting on one's career choice many years later, there seem to have been few clues as to how the decision was made, and when recalled, may not have been based on anything very practical. My principal recollection is of a *Life Magazine* article read as a teenager about an American lawyer, John Foster Dulles, partner in the Manhattan law firm of Sullivan and Cromwell, who was pictured traveling to airports, disembarking from airplanes, all accompanied by text describing him as a very important "international lawyer". I could not understand what such a person did but it sounded very interesting and that goal remained with me for a while; until a year or so later, when I got taken with the idea of becoming an "aeronautical engineer" based on some article I had read; and so it went. No consistency at all. Having been born in the midst of the depression, the only child of Hungarian immigrant parents, I had little idea of what awaited me in life. I understood that my parents wanted me to do well at school, so I studied hard, but also never missed opportunities to play whenever possible. We seemed to have enough money to lead a comfortable, middle class life. The rest of the world I had little to do with, except for the occasional intrusions of my mother's family members.

1

A World I Never Thought I Could Master

February 1931—that's when I arrived in this world, smack in the middle of the worst depression the USA had ever experienced.

I was born in The Bronx, New York, to Jewish parents who learned to speak and write English at night school and worked endless hours to make ends meet and to build up a savings account at the Bank of the United States. All this I learned by the time I became five by listening at the dinner table. At that same table I also acquired a conversational knowledge of the Hungarian language, for when my mother's parents were present, the language of the table became Hungarian. So it was that I became able to speak conversational Hungarian never having learned to read or write the language.

Some fifty years later, on a trip to Europe where I spent five days in Budapest with my future wife, I discovered that the language had remained buried somewhere in my subconscious because upon alighting from the plane and seeing a Currency Exchange kiosk, I went up to it and with no difficulty proceeded to change some dollars into Hungarian currency, and later was able to order meals in restaurants, and make small talk with store merchants.

While family discourse was mostly in Hungarian, I don't mean to suggest that my grandparents couldn't speak English. They could and did; but they preferred their native tongue, and among strangers it was a safe way to keep from being overheard by nosy gossips. My mother's father was an authority figure to me, constantly smoking cigars, often unlit and dangling from his lips, paying no attention at all to little children, and seeming to have little interest in the business of selling groceries, which was what he did for a living, being the sole proprietor of a small grocery store in The Bronx. But his was a loud voice, and my cousins and I were all afraid of displeasing him. I later found out what his real interest was: it was gambling, almost any kind.

Poker was played regularly by most of the adults in the family—and for money—on Sunday afternoons. But I also thought I overheard my grandfather speaking on the telephone in the grocery store, making bets with bookies at the racetrack. I found out for sure one day when the store was left in charge of his son, my Uncle Sam, and all of the rest of us except for my father, traveled out to a racetrack on Long Island. Every adult except my grandfather went to the ticket windows before each race and placed small bets—either $2 or $5—and cheered loudly for their horse to win while the race was on. But my grandfather did not bet—at first. Apparently, he had been banned from doing so any more by my grandmother. He waited until the second or third race, and while the others were busy placing their bets for the next race, he whispered to me that he had an important job for me. He sent me to a ticket window far from where they were, having given me five $10 bills and told me to tell the man behind the ticket window "All on Number 3" in that race, to keep my mouth closed and to just hold on to the ticket stubs, and not to give them to him until later. In the later races the number of the horse would change, but not the result. He always lost.

As we left the track, when no one was looking, I slipped him all the stubs—and then watched him tear them into pieces and throw the pieces into a nearby trashcan. That secret remained between us and he never spoke to me about our partnership. I suppose he represented some of the things I could not understand about the world around me, and I was too afraid of him to ever ask any questions.

On one fateful day during that period I was accompanying my mother on her shopping duties when I spotted a toy that I had to have in a store window.

My mother said, "No, absolutely no! We have no money for things like that!"

I wouldn't budge and started crying. She shouted to a neighbor who was witnessing this street scene to call my grandfather whose store happened to be nearby, to come right away. Moments later, wearing his grocer's apron, he furiously shouted at me and told me to start moving immediately and to get home, and I probably set a new speed record in the process. My mother never had a problem like that with me ever again.

I also learned at the dinner table that my parents had left Europe in fear of growing anti-Semitism, as well as my father being motivated, along with his older brother, to avoid being conscripted into the Hungarian army which was preparing for another European war. My mother's parents brought her and her brother and sister (their entire family) but my father and his older brother came alone, leaving parents and a large number of children, most all of whom died at the hands of the Nazis, as we later discovered. My mother told me, with some bitterness, that on arriving in the States, her father had quickly found her a job in a sewing factory, turning out ladies' shirtwaists for ten hours each day, after which she would go to evening English classes. Her sister was treated similarly. She also told me about the Triangle Shirt Factory fire, which had killed so many immigrant girls and women.

At the dinner table the American hero of most conversations I was able to understand was someone called "FDR". I wasn't sure who that was, but I soon figured out he was also called—somewhat in awe—"President Roosevelt". That this depression caused some terrible suffering—many people without jobs, without homes, and without food, also came to me at the dinner table. But most often, I heard the story of how all of my parents' hard-earned savings—deposited in the Bank of the United States—had been lost when that bank closed its doors with thousands standing in line for long hours in hope of some miracle that would return their life savings to them. It never happened and my parents had no understanding of how banks could "fail". So, they started saving all over again from scratch.

My father ran his own butcher store in The Bronx in partnership with his brother, which was not a happy relationship. At my grandfather's store, I was occasionally pressed into service as a delivery boy after school hours when I reached six years of age. I finished school at three each afternoon and was told to go to grandpa's store in case some old lady needed help in carrying her groceries home. While waiting for one of these tasks I played with my baseball cards or hopscotched on the sidewalk in front of the store. Sometimes, I might get lucky by being asked to help a lady who did not live very far away and whose parcels weren't too heavy for me, especially since most people lived in walk-up apartments. The payoff was when I got an occasional tip—usually a penny. Memories linger over the thrill of racing, accompanied by a couple of my scavenger pals, to the nearby candy store with that penny. It could buy an amazing assortment of small candies, which I would select by pointing to them through the glass showcase, and receiving them in a small paper bag from the candy storeowner, in exchange for my penny.

When I turned seven, a major change in our lives occurred. My father was offered an opportunity to buy his own store on Main Street in a place called "Flushing, New York" in the borough of Queens. Never heard of it, but the best part was he was able to leave his brother out of it. He was able to buy himself out of that partnership—by being substantially cheated by his brother. We moved out of The Bronx and into an apartment building on Franklin Street in Flushing and I was even happier than my mother and father. Needless to say, my mother, who had extremely keen business instincts and determination, largely negotiated the departure from The Bronx and her family.

2

Being an Only Child

I didn't think much about not having any baby brothers or sisters, or, for that matter, older siblings. That just seemed to be the way it was.

My mother only spoke about it to me once when I was eight or nine, and she let slip that she had been pregnant a year earlier but had lost the child. Despite his great kindness, my father never spoke to me about anything personal.

When we moved to Flushing, I liked the neighborhood a lot. Not only was it not crowded like The Bronx, but the open lots and fields were ideal for kids to turn into baseball diamonds, touch football fields, fireplaces for roasting *mickies* (potatoes), and the like. Everyone said that not long ago there had been cows and horses grazing in these fields, and it still had the feel of the country.

But I had no permanent friend to play with, just intermittent pickups that didn't last. The result was that I made up my own games, created imaginary friends, named them after characters in books that I read, and actually never seemed to feel lonely. I skipped third grade and by the time I turned eight I was in the fourth grade. The war in

Europe began to captivate my attention, as well as that of many of my schoolmates. One of the things I did was to volunteer to become an aircraft spotter for the plane-spotting group at the local "Y". We learned to identify American as well as German airplanes from their silhouettes, with the thought that we would one day become qualified airplane spotters.

One of the hobbies I developed was melting pieces of lead pipe I found on the lots in a small iron pot on our kitchen stove and pouring the molten lead into molds that someone had given me as a gift for making "tin" soldiers. My mother kept an eye on me when I was using the stove. I carefully painted the soldiers with the paints that came with the model-making kits. I also carefully carved balsa wood parts into wings, tails, cockpits, and propellers and eventually into accurate models of WW II fighter planes, which I brought to my plane-spotting group.

I went through the threat of having to play a musical instrument with relative ease. My mother proposed violin lessons for me. After two disastrous meetings with the instructress, who came to our apartment, my mother was advised not to proceed with my musical career. I had a similar experience at school. While I got only A's or excellent in all standard courses, when it came time for

Music Appreciation class, and I attempted to sing with the rest of the class, the teacher stood next to me listening one morning, then leaned down to me and whispered "Bobby, you're going to be a listener here." And that pretty much described my musical inability to carry a tune, or to appreciate the opera or classical music. I regretted it but had no control, as I appeared to be musically tone deaf. I consoled myself by playing sports and making model planes and soldiers.

By the time I was eleven, the United States had suffered Pearl Harbor and had declared war against Japan; Hitler had obliged FDR by declaring war on the USA; and I had joined the local Boy Scout Troop that met once a week in the basement of the local synagogue. My parents happily bought the Scout uniform for me, pleased that this was the only kind of uniform their son would be wearing. It was there that I befriended Don Holden, a boy my age, who had also skipped as many grades as I had, and was in my class at P.S. 20, our local grammar school.

A short while after our first meeting Don and I started visiting at each other's apartments after school, and we soon became such close friends that I believed that I had a brother. On Saturdays, we sometimes took subway trips into Manhattan, when, for five cents each way, we were able to line up outside the NBC Radio Studios in Rockefeller Center to become part of the live audience for a quiz show or a soap opera. On the Saturdays when we had more money in our pockets, we would park ourselves in the local Flushing Loews or RKO Keith's movie house, children's section, at 10 o'clock in the morning. We would sit there most of the day, watching the double feature movies, at least twice, along with our favorite cowboy serial, where the hero was always on the brink of death, that is, until the next Saturday when we could watch him miraculously evade the landslide or train wreck that ended the prior week's episode. My mother never failed to bring a brown bag lunch for both of us. We sat glued to our chairs while the matron located us in the darkened movie house.

Don and I remained extremely close throughout both grammar school and Flushing High School, co-authoring a humor column for the school paper in high school, in which we reprinted many jokes and stories that we lifted from our readings—from Groucho Marx to Mark Twain—or joke books that we found. We also enjoyed comparing ideas from the various novels we read in our separate English classes, and finally we talked a lot about the different colleges to which we thought of applying. Interestingly, there was never any question that we were going to go to college, while I would say that the same was true for only a smallish number of our classmates, perhaps ten percent of our class.

Eventually, Don told me that he could only apply to Columbia College in Manhattan, as his parents wanted him to remain in New York City and live at home. I pointed out how he was going to miss all of the fun of campus life as described in the books that we had read, but he said he had no choice. Meanwhile, my mother and I discussed which colleges I should apply to many times. She said that she did not ever want to hold me back from getting ahead and going where I thought it best for me. But she always pointed out that she didn't know anything about colleges, so I had to figure it out myself.

I had read many books about Harvard and what life was like in Cambridge, Massachusetts, and was taken in by the college's claim to be the best in the country. My history teacher had also gone there and offered to write a recommendation for me. I remembered that I also had a second cousin, who I saw very rarely, who was entering her junior year at the University of Michigan in Ann Arbor, Michigan; she urged me to apply, saying it was a great school, and I should get away from my parents' control, as she had done from hers. I discussed Michigan with my mother, without mentioning my cousin's reasoning and she thought it might be a good idea to apply. So Harvard and Michigan it became, with Syracuse thrown in as a fail-safe, though I had absolutely no desire to go there.

My rejection by Harvard came as a surprise. I had excellent SAT scores, was third in my graduating class academically and had been skipped three grades. But Harvard had a question about religion on its application, which the other schools did not. Only years later did I learn of the 5% quota on the admission of Jewish students that existed at certain Ivy League Schools. I was sixteen when I was accepted at Michigan, and although I had been accepted by Syracuse, which was much closer, my mother told me that I could go to Michigan even though it was 750 miles away. But she wanted to accompany me on my first trip out there to make sure that I had a nice room, to meet my roommates, and to see the school. She came with me on the train and we had a lovely trip.

Don Holden and I corresponded with each other at first, but his efforts petered out by the close of our freshman year. We lost track of each other, apart from occasional gossip from mutual friends, which was how I learned that he had married Wilma Shafer, who lived across the street from me and was a year behind us at Flushing High.

Amazingly, we renewed our friendship again when we were in our seventies. I learned that he'd had a career in publishing, then museum work, and then and now as an artist, living in Irvington, New York. He learned that I had become a successful international lawyer, and was now semi-retired and living in Lakeville, Connecticut. I never did have an adult male friendship as close as that childhood one, though marriage served as an effective replacement.

3

College at Michigan

Due to the return of GIs from WW II and the "GI Bill
of Rights," there were three of us in an East Quadrangle
room designed for two. I chose the upper bunk in the room
since I didn't like the idea of someone stepping on me as
they stumbled into bed late at night. My lower bunkmate,
Hal, a short, skinny kid from Grosse Point near Detroit, was
rich, lazy, and somewhat annoying. He started on me as
soon as we met.

"How many cashmere sweaters do you have?" he
asked.

Not exactly sure what a cashmere sweater was, I said I
didn't know.

"How can you not know? Show me the sweaters you
brought with you."

Upon inspecting the sweaters I brought, he scoffed,
"Those two rags aren't cashmere; they're just plain wool,
and pretty worn out. You should go to Hudson's in Detroit
and buy yourself a really good cashmere sweater; that's
what the girls like to see; also the frat brothers when you try
to pledge a good frat."

I didn't grasp all that he was rattling on about and

16

didn't care about anything he thought important. I told him that I had no interest in fraternities; that I'd come to Michigan to learn and wanted to get good grades. Also I had little extra money, so I asked that he please leave me alone about my sweaters. He paid no attention.

"I have eight cashmeres and already told the brothers at ZBT about them during pledge week, which you apparently missed."

"I didn't miss it. I have no interest at all in any of them. So no more talk about them or your sweaters, please!"

Hal also played poker somewhere most evenings and for a while kept inviting me to join him; but I was finally able to convince him that I had no money to squander on poker losses. Since I wasn't as good a student as he must be to have all that time for poker, I needed my time to study. He didn't get my sarcasm and thankfully dropped the subject.

Our other roommate was another story entirely. His name was Mel, was from Flint, in upper Michigan, at least ten years older than I was (16 1/2), had a dark beard, and weighed in at close to 200 pounds. A WW II veteran, Mel said he was an economics major and was serious about getting good grades.

One morning early in the semester he took a look at

me—I was about 5' 11' and 170 pounds, and looked fairly strong—and said: "Kid, you're coming with me to the Campus Bookstore this morning."

"Why, Mel?" I asked.

"You'll see," he replied. And off we went, me trying to keep up with his long strides.

At the store, he bought some Economics texts, which did not surprise me, and then headed over to the medical textbooks, which were big and very thick. He bought a bunch of those, paying for everything with a kind of voucher from his G.I. Bill.

I asked: "Mel, what are you doing buying all these medical textbooks; besides weighing a ton, they're very expensive. And you're an econ major, you told us, right?"

"Yup," he responded. "Now just carry the books and don't drop any. You'll see why tomorrow."

They were very heavy, which made the return trip to the dorm quite unpleasant.

The next morning he said to me: "OK, kid. We're goin' back to the bookstore. You carry half these medical books and I'll take the rest."

Puzzled, I followed orders and watched as he went to the Book Return counter at the store. I heard him explain to the clerk that somehow his wife (which he didn't have) had made a mistake in typing up the books he needed so he was returning them. He showed his receipts for having bought them through the G.I. Bill and the clerk proceeded to give him some $200 in cash for the returned books.

He said to me: "Now maybe you can learn some economics from this. Our brilliant government lets me pay for books with its paper, but when the books get returned, the bookstore pays me cash. So that's why I buy the most expensive books in the store—medical textbooks! Since you're having the fun of helping me get some cash, I don't even charge you for the pleasure of watching the scheme!" That was Mel. He did study hard, and moved out to another dorm to join some of his ex-GI friends at the end of the semester.

My first year grades turned out to be all A's, so I was elected to the Freshman Honor Society. My parents were very pleased, as was I. The only thing that was not going well was my social life, which can only be described as non-existent. The girls in my classes were mostly 17 or 18 and wouldn't even glance at anyone as young as me. Besides, I was extremely shy. For six months I never got up the nerve to ask the cute girl sitting next to me in PoliSci class for a "coke date", the standard afternoon social activity at the Michigan Union.

Eating at the East Quad dining hall, I became friends with a classmate from Detroit named Norman Brock, who agreed with all of my complaints about the food. We started eating together in town for Sunday lunch, as the dining hall was closed for that one meal each week. Our favorite eatery was The Old German restaurant in downtown Ann Arbor where we rarely changed our menu choice of wiener schnitzel, mashed potatoes and green peas, with a stein of excellent German beer.

When second semester began after the mid-year Holiday break, dear old Hal did not appear. The word was that he had flunked out in style, not getting a passing grade in any of his courses. Too bad for him that they didn't give a course in poker playing.

I had spotted an ad on a bulletin board for Summer Camp counselors at something called "Pioneer Youth Camp" in upstate New York, which had Mrs. Eleanor Roosevelt listed as one of its sponsors. I applied for a summer job there, was accepted and had a good summer. Many of the boys were from troubled families and I had the experience of both helping them adjust to the outdoor life of living in a tent and befriending them. Often I felt quite sorry for them but directed my efforts to trying to keep their spirits high.

The following year at Michigan, I was back in the East Quad. Largely due to the dining hall food, Norm Brock and I decided to pledge a fraternity, Kappa Nu, which was known to serve very good food. Its members were mostly pre-meds and had excellent grades. I ran into Economics 101 that semester and encountered my first "B".

Since I wanted to earn some extra money for clothes (sport jacket, slacks, and a winter coat for the extremely cold Michigan winters), I answered an ad on the dorm bulletin board for a student willing to read textbooks to a WW II veteran I'll call Allen, who had been blinded in combat. He was an extremely intelligent student, married to a lovely woman; most important, he was an English major, which I was well on my way to becoming, so I was reading aloud novels, poetry and only occasionally, history texts. They lived in a Quonset hut building, as did many married veterans. Allen had to transfer for personal reasons after the first semester, but I have never forgotten the pleasure of that experience.

Kappa Nu was all Jewish and quite a disappointment. My pledge weeks were awful, except for the excellent meals served by non-Jewish student athletes on scholarships. On the last night of pledging—called Hell Night—I was driven, blindfolded, some twenty miles outside of Ann Arbor, and dumped outside of the car without a dime on me, and told to be back at the fraternity house by morning. Somehow I made it back, already starting to doubt the wisdom of this entire fraternity involvement. The following night I was elected as a Brother, and also told that I had been selected as Pledgemaster for the new crop of pledges to the organization for the next semester. I tried to turn it down but they wouldn't allow me to, and told me what an honor the job was!

My first taste of being Pledgemaster turned me strongly against the officers of this organization. It was during Pledge Week that many prospective new members were invited to mixers at the House. The Brothers looked over the crop and made decisions as to whom they would like to invite to be pledges. Many of those decisions were easy. But I noticed one freshman who appeared entirely ill at ease and unsuited for fraternity life. Harvey was his name and he arrived by bicycle, didn't wear a jacket, only a sweater and a bow tie. He was obviously a science whiz and headed for the Engineering School. I knew he was wrong for this group and said so after the first mixer. The older members mumbled about needing a full pledge class: they said Harvey might be a necessary choice for financial reasons. I argued to the Officers that I could not believe they would accept him as a pledge just to get his money. They ignored me and voted to offer him a place in the new pledge class, which, of course, was under my supervision.

Everything went as I predicted. Harvey was a terrible pledge; very earnest and serious, but awkward at meeting new people, chatting with visiting alumni on football Saturdays, or whatever they wanted him to do. His Class all survived their Hell Night, including Harvey, and I suspected what was going to happen. At the meeting to vote in the new members from his pledge class, three of the older members voted to blackball Harvey. I was outraged and spoke up.

"I told you not to pledge him as we all knew he was awkward and not a joiner, but you wanted his money and now you're willing to slam the door in his face after he has put up with all of your bullshit for six weeks. Well, go ahead and do it! Blackball him! I won't continue as a member of this group. You'll have my written resignation in the morning and I'll be moving out as soon as I can find an apartment on campus."

The next morning I wrote my letter of resignation and gave it to the President, a bit of a coward, who told me how sorry he was to lose me, but asked if we couldn't work something out.

"Like what?" I asked.

He replied, "Like you take your meals here and pay for them. You know how good the food is, and we need the money. But you don't have to live here or participate in our other activities."

"I'll try it out," I said.

That night I had to tell Harvey he had been blackballed, and added that I was terribly embarrassed by the conduct of the Brothers. He, of all things, asked if I could help him find them in their bedrooms so he could say goodbye. I found it hard to believe, but I helped him do it. We tracked them down one by one, hiding as best they could from Harvey, who wouldn't skip any of them. I told him as we finished, that I wished him luck in his studies and hoped to see him around the Quadrangle or at the Student Union in the future.

Meanwhile, I rented a small room in a nearby boarding house that served no meals, and paid the fraternity to eat lunch and dinner there, being on my own for breakfast. It really was a good deal for me. I would have been charged at least that amount if I had stayed in the East Quad, and I knew these guys were in financial straits so I could get away with a lot. But I really did not care for any of them very much at all, except that I remained very friendly with Norm Brock.

During the academic year, I tried out for the college newspaper, The Michigan Daily, where I was eventually assigned to cover the Law School—not an exciting posting—when I did not make the Editorial Board. But on election eve 1948, when Dewey was running against Truman, I had been on late "putting the paper to bed" duty and went to my room at around midnight when Truman appeared to be losing badly. I was awakened by my landlady telling me there was a phone call for me, which turned out to be the Night Editor of the paper telling me to get back immediately as Truman was making a huge comeback. By the time I arrived at the printing plant, Truman, with the farm vote pouring in, had a slight lead. By daylight he had won and I bought myself a paper with the headline "DEWEY BEATS TRUMAN" as a souvenir.

I also tried out for the Tennis Team, but missed there too, and remained on the Tennis Squad, a group of potential substitutes in case *every* Team member was injured or ill.

Over the next summer I found myself a job at the New York City Main Library on Fifth Avenue at 42nd Street, microfilming their index cards from the Main Reading Room in the event of an atomic attack or air raids that they were worried about. It allowed me to live at my parent's home, taking the subway to work each day; I liked my fellow *microfilmers* and enjoyed the summer.

In my junior year I made the decision to become an English major and applied to the English Honors Program, which accepted me. But I ran into the requirement of having to take at least one laboratory science course prior to graduation, and with some bad luck, fell into an Astronomy Class that resulted in my first college C+.

I was assigned an advisor in the Honors Program and we hit it off quite well. My favorite English professor, Mr. Barrett, was not allowed to be my advisor. My new advisor notified me of a scholarship being offered by the International Education Institute for summer study at Balliol College, Oxford, England in 19th Century English literature, which included all transportation, tuition, and a modest living allowance. I applied with his recommendation and was selected for the summer program. After consulting my parents, who, as usual, told me to take the opportunity, I wound up sailing on the Queen Mary in 3rd class to England in late July of 1950.

On the ship, I made friends with two colleagues who were part of the same program. Gurston Goldin, a History major from Columbia College, and Mac Katz, a third year student at the Yale Law School, who had gone to Wisconsin prior to Yale. We hit it off quite well. Gurston had an uncanny ability to master the ship's alleyways and staircases so that he led us from our 3rd Class area into First Class repeatedly. Only the requirement of black tie garb kept us out of First Class every evening. While other passengers suffered seasickness and missed many meals, that was not a problem for us and we thrived on the excellent fare served even in 3rd Class.

On arrival in England and journeying to Oxford, I found the Bursar's Office at Balliol locked tight until a week later and had to fend for myself with very little money until it did open. So I rented a bicycle and joined a Youth Hostel organization where I found cheap accommodations each night if I could cycle the distance to the next hostel before it shut down for the night. Once I slept out under the stars in a sleeping bag and another time, had to rent a cheap room in the outskirts of London; but I survived until the Balliol bursary reopened.

England was still recuperating from the shortages of WW II and starting to enjoy the benefits of the Marshall Plan, but for the food served at the Dining Hall at Balliol, there was only one word: awful; cold spaghetti on toast, for example. Mac Katz introduced me to the rest of his Yale

Law chums who were there essentially for a summer vacation. They were Richard N. Gardner, incoming Articles and Book Review Editor of the Yale Law Journal, Bill Wolff, a wealthy bon vivant, Ellis Manning, a charming representative from the South; there was also a dour fellow who was the new Editor-in-Chief of the Harvard Law Review, who was not friendly with any of us. They made clear to me that there was a sharp difference between the Harvard and Yale Law schools which was not known by many people. They explained that Harvard had an entering class of close to 500 and flunked out over one hundred by end of first year. Yale, on the other hand, only accepted an entering class of about 165, none of which were ever flunked out. If they quit, it was their own choice, but mostly all graduated. They also lived in the law quadrangle, where they ate and studied, unless they happened to be married. They strongly advised me that if I decided to go to law school, *choose Yale*. At the time, I was still contemplating an academic career as a professor of English. Still, I appreciated their advice about Yale, which I had never heard of previously, except for the movie *Adam's Rib*, starring Spencer Tracy and Katherine Hepburn.

The academic experience at Balliol, for me, was exceptional. Used to gigantic lecture courses at Michigan, I was delighted by the Tutorial system at Oxford. I met with a small group of students in the rooms of our Tutor once each week, where we discussed papers written by members at an earlier time. Then we were off to the Library to do research and prepare a short paper on a subject suggested by the Tutor.

When I went off to the Bodleian Library, I was able to simply wander through the stacks, take down any book I cared to look at, and sign it out for a week or so, which resulted in my getting interested in many subjects in addition to the paper of my assignment. The discussions were at a very high level and of great enjoyment to me. I suspected that my Yale Law friends had a very poor attendance record at their tutorials.

Dick Gardner and I became friendly due to a weekend trip that we took when we discovered that we each liked the poetry of W. H. Auden and were interested in visiting the area that he wrote about. We hiked and read in the land of Auden and got to know each other somewhat; and we saw each other over the years both in New York and Washington, when our bar association lives brought us together.

On my return to Ann Arbor, one of the first things I did was to head for the Main Reading Room of the Library and inquire if there was a way of looking through the stacks for books I might be interested in. The Head Librarian explained that what I was asking for was called a Stack Pass and that it was only available to faculty or to members of Honors Programs. I explained that I was a member of the English Honors program. She then gave me an application form to have filled out by the Program Administrator after which I could be given my Stack Pass, which I received in a matter of days. What a difference it made in my research and general reading experience! I could be routinely seen coming out of the stacks with a pile of books each time I was there, taking them all out; sometimes returning many of them quickly after they had satisfied my curiosity. I was delighted and realized how much was lost by students who did not have such privileges.

The Korean War had broken out in 1950 and many graduating seniors were being drafted. I was now in my senior year and it was the spring of 1951. I had already, at my Honors advisor's urging, applied for a Teaching Fellowship in English at the University of Connecticut, which I was virtually assured of receiving. Harry Truman, bless his soul, came out with a Student Deferment Program, which applied to all kinds of schools, including medicine, law, and some others, but not English literature.

As the idea of being shot at in freezing temperatures by North Koreans or Chinese did not appeal to me, and since I never had anything to do with the campus ROTC activities, I quickly sent for the application forms for seven law schools, Yale being my first choice based on the advice I had received at Oxford. I picked up a Michigan application immediately, dropped it off, and was accepted soon thereafter, but did not want another three years in the winters of Ann Arbor. Yale also accepted me fairly quickly, my final year's grades being all A's again, and graduating with Honors in English. Harvard also accepted me and I had the pleasure of turning them down, in partial repayment of their having rejected my college application ostensibly due to their Jewish quota at the time.

I accepted the Yale offer by return mail, and arranged for my Draft Board to know that I qualified for a student deferment under the new law.

4

Career Advice in College

As I'd grown up reading as many books as I could, I noticed that many of the stories and movies that I enjoyed most were about lawyers, such as the Scopes trial and Clarence Darrow, Atticus Finch and *To Kill a Mockingbird*, and Earl Stanley Gardner's *Perry Mason*. So it is not strange that I gave some early thought to becoming a lawyer when I grew up.

I mentioned this idea to my mother while I was still in college. She didn't like it very much as she was a Jewish mother, for whom the ideal son became a doctor. And I could not help but notice that all of my smarter Jewish classmates were "pre-med" with a vengeance. They would kill for an A in Chemistry. Meanwhile, I felt faint at the sight of blood and was a zero at lab science subjects, only completing the required science classes by taking mathematics, which I liked and got A's in, and a required laboratory science course in Astronomy. But that is where my undoing came. I had been told by one and all that Astronomy was a "gut" course that many of what were then, the Rose Bowl Champion, Michigan football team members took, in order to qualify for their degrees, from a dizzy lady professor; and they got mostly A's or B's. So when I registered I saw there was an astronomy class at 8 a.m. and another at 10 a.m. That was an easy choice and I thought nothing about picking the 10 a.m. class. When I entered the room on the first day of the class there was not a football player in sight. Nor was the professor female. On later inquiry I learned that the team were all in the 8 a.m. section, and no one had warned me about that. Thus, I got my first C+ as a Michigan honors student.

Prior to the start of my junior year, I was accepted into the English Department's Honors program and seemed to be heading toward becoming a college professor, but I still had an unfinished idea of what it might be like to become a lawyer. When I talked to my mother about this, she was understanding but said that unfortunately she was unable to give me any advice and that I should talk to her real estate lawyer, Frank Guarino, during a school vacation, to ask for his advice about going to law school instead of graduate school, as he was the only lawyer my family knew.

At the time she was heavily engaged in buying, fixing up, and flipping houses—a business at which she was making a fair amount of extra income, and she used only Frank for her deals as he was knowledgeable and very honest. So, during Spring Vacation from Ann Arbor I phoned Frank as she advised, and he immediately asked me to come to his office on Main Street in Flushing, just one floor above the local Queens County Savings Bank branch and in the next building to the offices of the Local Selective Service Board, which had already started bothering me with post cards about taking a physical exam. I told him that one of the things I had been thinking about after college was law school if I decided against graduate school in English, and needed some advice as no one in my family had even gone to college, let alone become a lawyer.

Frank was extraordinarily kind to me, said he couldn't give me much advice since I was obviously a good student and would probably be able to gain admission to and graduate from one of the very top law schools, while he had only attended night school at St. Johns in Brooklyn while working during the day. But he did say that there was one piece of solid advice he could give me if I decided to make my career as a lawyer. It went as follows:

"The law business is nothing like the real estate business or in fact, any other business, but you can make a decent, comfortable living, but never be able to accumulate enough money to live really well. Just put some of the yearly after tax income you will earn as a lawyer aside—in a bank account—until an opportunity comes along to invest in real estate; hold what you buy for several years or more, and if you bought well, you should be able to sell it at a large profit, be taxed only as capital gains, and would then have enough capital to make a larger purchase—commercial stores, a house, an apartment, part of a shopping center—but always making a substantial profit--just like your mother does."

I thanked him very much for the advice, which, by the way, I put into practice in later years without regret. On my return to Ann Arbor, I remained in the English Honors program, only keeping my interest in law alive by covering the Michigan Law School for the college newspaper—until the Korean War broke out! Draft notices were flying thick and fast, but President Harry S. Truman, as noted earlier, came up with an outrageously undemocratic Student Draft Deferment Act; going to law school, medical school, and certain engineering schools, entitled a student to a deferment until graduation. However, ordinary graduate school to become a PhD, leading to a teaching career, got you drafted and off to Korea. I immediately applied to seven different law schools; all of my applications were accepted and I was on my way to New Haven, Connecticut in the fall after my graduation, for at least three years of draft-deferred legal studies.

5

On Arriving at the Yale Law School— September 1951

The first thing that needs to be said about arriving at this august and revered law school was that many long-held beliefs had been passed over for the entering class that would graduate in May of 1954. We learned this the hard way. In the main law school auditorium for our introductory welcome by Dean Wesley Sturges, it seemed that the size of the group was much too large. For decades the school was known for its small, selective class size— somewhere around 160 to 165, tops. The advantages were obvious: small classes, more opportunity for faculty attention, and more accessibility to job opportunity on graduation. Here it was obvious that the size of my new class was over 200 easily. We later were informed that the actual number was 217.

The explanation was quite simple, if not entirely satisfactory: The Korean War. The Administration of the school apparently had been very concerned that the universal draft would wipe out many, if not most, of those admitted. It, therefore, decided to admit an unusually large number of freshmen into the first-year class, dropping its academic and other standards low enough so as to secure well over 200 acceptances, all of whom quickly chose Yale over their other law school acceptances. Now, it was true that this statute was the incentive for many of us to apply to law school, but I, for one, never expected that Yale Law School would alter its admissions standards in order to make certain that it had enough seats filled—tuition paid—to carry on as though nothing had been changed. Once the law was enacted, and the acceptance letters sent, the die was cast. To this day, I remember how soon I had received my Yale acceptance letter after applying. Our class would have many members who would never have been admitted under the normal peacetime standards, some of whom I knew.

One fellow was from my own undergraduate school—the University of Michigan. He was lazy, not all that bright, but shrewd, a member of the *Sigma Alpha Mu* fraternity, who repeatedly turned up on my doorstep a day or two before final exams in PoliScience, History, or Literature classes, in his bright red Cadillac convertible, to borrow notes, none of which he had bothered taking during the course term. I acceded, because I didn't care what grades he got. In my view, we were in two different universes. And of all things, I saw his smiling face among the 217 sitting in the auditorium awaiting the Dean's introductory welcome to the new Yale Law School class of 1954. When we chatted later that afternoon about the coincidence of meeting in New Haven, he readily admitted that he was not at first accepted by Yale Law School but received a second letter stating that if he wished to journey to New Haven for a personal interview, there was some chance he might be admitted. He did so and by the force of his obnoxious personality, was now one of my classmates, again!

As classes began, the major change that was thrown at us, one which terrified me, was the Socratic method, by which concepts were explored by rigorous cross-examining of one student by the professor for a substantial period of time while others raised their hands to fill in the obvious errors of the attacked designated responder. At each class most of us either sat lower in our seats, changed seats in order to fool the seating chart, or took our chances at not being called upon. It was an exercise that most of us disliked, but were compelled to live by. One wag made kind of a name for himself when he was called upon by Professor J. W. Moore to "State the case of *Erie Railroad v. Tompkins*", and responded politely that he had not read it. The professor was visibly surprised but moved on to query another student about a different case. Two days later, when the class next met, Moore called on that same student.

"Well, Mr. Malkin, have you now had the opportunity since we last met to read the *Erie Railroad* case?"

Malkin replied, "Yes, sir. I have."

Everyone breathed a sigh of relief.

"Well, please state the case for us, sir."

Malkin responded, "I did have the *opportunity* to read it sir, but I didn't take advantage of it," causing a great gasp from the class, along with several outsized bursts of laughter. Professor Moore simply shook his head in mild disgust and moved on to another victim.

But the pressure of this new kind of classroom interrogation did take its toll. I, for one, was very nervous about speaking in public and never was relaxed in any of my classes until I heard the bell ring. Whether the Socratic method was an effective mode of teaching is a question that is still being debated, but many law schools have abandoned it for reasons known to them only. Some years later, when I taught an entering freshman section of the Contracts course at Stanford Law School, I never used it.

6

End of First Year at Yale Law School

My first semester law school grades were good enough to relax my discipline of studying every night until midnight or later, and when one of my chums, Matt, suggested a Saturday afternoon trip to Vassar for a Hillel Society mixer, I readily agreed. I still had my father's old Buick, parked in a nearby garage during the week, which made me popular among the girl-happy set. Matt had little interest in law school; he saw the opportunity before us as marrying a very rich girl from one of the Seven Sister Colleges; her family would then hire him in some executive slot and introduce him to a life of luxury. I couldn't have disagreed with him more, and we really weren't close, but he was handsome, glib, and, I thought, a great finder of pretty girls, while I was still kind of shy with them.

He had told me that the mixer at the Vassar Hillel Society on Saturday evening would be a great way to meet some girls without having to spend any money, except for the gas for the car. I was fine with that and off we drove to Poughkeepsie late one Saturday afternoon in the spring of our first year. As it was my first trip to Vassar, I got a little lost for a while. Matt was not much help with driving directions. By the time we finally found the College, we had missed the mixer. As we walked into the building where it had been held, some girls and guys were just coming out. Matt went to see if anything else might be going on, while I kept walking toward the girls who were leaving. One of them came up to me and politely asked if I needed directions. I will never forget how she looked: dark hair, deep brown eyes, extremely pretty face, dressed in a long tartan skirt, white sox, and saddle shoes—kind of a Fifties Vassar uniform.

"Is there any place where my friend and I could get something to eat?" I said, trying to make conversation.

"My dorm's dining room will be opening in a little while and I'd be happy to invite you there as a guest. I'm allowed two guests on the weekends."

I was captivated by her looks, her friendliness, and her thoughtfulness.

All I could mumble was, "Could I bring my friend along?"

"Certainly," she said. "Where is he?"

"Over there, reading the bulletin board," I said.

We walked over to Matt. I still had the brains to introduce myself.

She replied: "I'm Janet, Janet Binder. I'm a freshman

here," she said.

I introduced him and told him of our invitation to the dining hall, which he quickly agreed to. Actually, I was wishing he were *not* there. I was already smitten. What a lovely, kind girl! And I had Matt to drag along, who I knew only cared about her father's business portfolio or contacts he could make. We opened the line at the cafeteria in Main House, the freshmen dormitory then, and had quite a nice, simple meal, which I knew Matt would bitch about.

When the meal was over, we decided to start back, since the drive took at least an hour and a half. Route 9 was curvy and it was getting dark. I arranged to speak to Janet alone before we shoved off, got her telephone number and asked if I could call her the coming Monday evening. She looked pleased and warned me that the number was of a phone in the corridor of the dorm and there would be a wait while someone called her to the phone. I said, "No problem," and got in the car already planning to ask her out for dinner the following Saturday night, sans Mr. Matt.

Back at school, I kept away from Matt but I was interested in finding a companion for the drive and told a couple of friends of my good luck. One of them bit, very hard. Bob Lewis was a wise guy from the University of Alabama, who had been in the same Jewish college fraternity as I had been at Michigan. We had met each other several days before school began while examining some Ivy League clothes in the Langrock store at the center of the Yale Campus. The owner had promised us a one-third discount on anything we bought there if we would tell our classmates how much we liked the Langrock cut and fit, and we had accepted the deal. Every time we convinced one of our classmates to buy a new jacket or suit at Langrock's, we told them to mention our names. We had done very well on the deal, which had resulted in an almost new wardrobe for me.

Lewis wanted me to get him a blind date. I said I would try, but if Janet were willing to fix him up, he would have to promise me to behave properly. He seemed to have a chip on his shoulder because of being a Jew in the South. At school, he liked to sit down at a table in the dining hall and say "Tell me what it's like living in *New Yawk* with all those liberals," a quip which he knew would cause trouble, often resulting in new classmates changing tables, if inadvertently seated next to him. He promised to behave, and I foolishly believed him.

I phoned Janet on Monday evening, waited on the line until she was called to the phone, and found her most willing to go out with me for dinner on Saturday evening.

When I raised the subject of a blind date, she was hesitant.

"What's he like?" she asked.

"OK", I lied, "He's Jewish, went to the University of Alabama, and likes to tell jokes."

She reluctantly agreed, saying that one of her roommates was a very pretty, but serious, student from the upper West Side of Manhattan.

"Aren't a lot of people from the South very prejudiced against Blacks?" she asked.

"I guess so, but I told him politics are off limits."

We went forward, making dinner plans at one of the roadhouse restaurants outside of Poughkeepsie, which also offered dancing. While dancing, Janet and I continued the brief exploration we had made the prior Saturday about both being interested in English literature. I told her about my having gotten into the Senior Honors English program at Michigan and she told me that she was planning to major in English as well. We both liked D.H. Lawrence, Jonathan Swift and Mark Twain, so our common interests were becoming clearer.

At dinner, Lewis disregarded every one of my warnings and began his inquiry into what it must be like to live on the Upper West Side amongst all those *lefties*. I got tired of kicking him under the table, and Janet's roommate very soon got tired of Lewis, and asked that we pay the check and return her to the dormitory, which I arranged to do. I let her out at the entrance to Main House, and Lewis insisted on walking her to the front door to say goodnight. I then parked the car in the parking area while I asked Janet if she would be my weekend date at an upcoming law school weekend dance. She agreed, I was thrilled, and walked her to the same front door to say goodnight. Suddenly, I heard a loud splash of water followed by a shout from Lewis. I ran around the building, where I encountered a soaked Lewis. When I asked him what was happening, he explained that he had ascertained from his date where her dorm window was located and had started throwing pebbles at her dorm window, in order, he said, to "kind of, serenade her". Apparently, that was the last thing in the world that she wanted. Opening her window, she had asked him to wait there for a moment, and returned with a bucket of very cold water, which she had heaved out the window onto his upturned face.

"And that's just for openers if you ever try to talk to me again," she yelled at him.

Lewis sheepishly climbed into my car and sat in silence as we headed back to New Haven, a two-hour drive. After a while, I let him know how he had deliberately engaged in the same inane inquiries that had caused classmates to avoid him in the law school and which he had promised me to avoid that night, imperiling my nascent romance. He mumbled an apology, saying he didn't understand why we Northerners were so touchy.

I simply replied, "Tonight is the last time we are going out socially while I'm at the law school. Having a meal in the dining room is as far as we socialize together from now on. Got it?"

The rest of the ride passed in silence. It turned out that he never came back to the law school, admitting to me in a phone call during the summer that he found the academics too difficult and was seeing a psychiatrist for his problems adjusting to school. He finished school at a local Birmingham law school and had a career as a plaintiff's negligence lawyer.

7

My Summer at the Norfolk Country Club

It had become the time when plans were being made for the summer. Some classmates were overly ambitious and bothered the Placement Office for interviews to work for a law firm as a summer clerk. My attitude was the inverse—no law books, but something outdoors with plenty of fresh air, and perhaps some fun, in addition to making some money, which I did need since I paid for my meals by working as a dishwasher in the school dining facility in order to use some of my father's allowance money for my social life. Janet had gotten a student teaching position at a NYC high school through her mother's connections and we realized that distance would most probably keep us apart until the fall semester.

The young lady in charge of the Placement Office said there were only two listings for outdoor jobs. One was on an estate in Port Washington, New York, complete with motor boat, sailboat, tennis court, where I would be the companion (watchdog) to two teenagers, twenty-four hours a day. Besides all meals and lodging, I would receive a stipend of $100 per week. This was the summer of 1952, and it sounded attractive, but boring.

"What's the other listing?" I asked.

"Well, I don't know if you play tennis well enough to be an instructor at the Norfolk Tennis Club in Norfolk, Connecticut. The pay is also $100 a week. The students are all young children of the members, and there is only a small room over the kitchen, next to the golf instructor's room, for you to stay in. But your meals are also included."

"I was on the Michigan tennis squad, not the team, in college, so I think I can handle the kids. I like tennis, so I would like to apply for the Norfolk job. How do I do it?" I said.

"Well, I will make an appointment for you to be interviewed by the Club president, at the Yale Club in New York City when he is next there, and he will decide if you're qualified." she said.

"Great. Just let me know when to go there," I replied.

A couple of days later she called me to say I should be at the Yale Club of NYC, right across the street from Grand Central Station at 2:00 p.m. the following Wednesday for my interview. She told me to dress nicely and to be relaxed because she had no one else applying.

That day I put on my best Langrock sport jacket, white-button down collar Brooks Brothers shirt, and striped repp tie, together with neatly pressed khaki trousers and shined penny loafers, and took the train in to Grand Central. I had been told to ask for my interviewer at the front Concierge Desk. "Right upstairs to the 3rd floor, the Tap Room. Just ask for him," I was told. In the Tap Room I was led to a window table where a lone gentleman about 55 years old, sat with two empty martini glasses in front of him, while he was sipping from a third. I introduced myself and was asked to pull up a chair and whether I would like a drink. I politely declined and the interview, if one could call it that, commenced.

"So you're at the Law School, is that right?

"Yes sir," I replied.

We chatted about the classes, his relatives who had gone to the College, how many years ago he had graduated from there, and so on.

"You know we can only pay $100 a week and the Club gets all the lesson income; the fellow who runs the Club is named Stackey, and he can tell you when to turn up and show you the room to use, and whatever else you need to know. Pleasure to meet you, son, and good luck."

Since he had no idea whether I could teach the game, and I didn't even know where Norfolk was, I figured we each came out pretty even. A day later I got the Club's phone number from the young woman at the Placement

Office. After I had spoken to Stackey, who told me how to get to Norfolk by car, he commented that I would probably have a splendid outdoors summer, which I did.

Before I left New Haven I received a phone call from a gentleman named Mike Blanchard, who said he was the Northeast Sales Rep for Spalding Sports equipment and had learned of my being hired for the Norfolk job.

"I can supply you with all the equipment that you will need—balls, rackets, shoes, shirts, shorts, sweaters, etc." he said.

"But Mr. Blanchard, I have no money to buy all that stuff; and the Club keeps all the lesson income."

"It's 'Mike', and of course I know you don't have any money now—you're a student. But I know the Norfolk families and have been supplying the Club's instructors for years. They made good money, as you will. Consignment—that's how we do business! I ship you all the stuff you'd like to sell and you pay me for the stuff you sell, after you've been paid your cost plus the mark-up you need to make some profit. Whatever you don't sell I take back at the end of the summer. Just verify what I think is the case—that Mr. Smith doesn't care what you do about selling stuff to members and their families, and we're in business!"

That's what I did. Mr. Smith said the Club's attitude hadn't changed and I was off to the races. Several kids came in my first week, signed up for lessons, and I talked them into balls, a couple of new rackets, and some tennis shirts. All they had to do was sign a chit after scribbling their parents' membership number on it, and I got a check from the Club every two weeks for their charges. The summer was very profitable for me.

My pupils during the week were the young sons and daughters of prominent New Yorkers such as Brendan Gill, the Websters (owners, I was told, of the American Tobacco Company), and similar members of the landed gentry. It turned out that the Norfolk Club members were all in *The Social Register*, and many owned large summer estates in the area. The husbands were in the City during the week and drove up for the weekend, when there was always a dinner dance on Saturday night. Many members had their own bottles with nametags on them at the bar, and I was always amazed at how they were able to drive home without getting killed or running over some innocent locals. Of course, that was none of my business. I often was asked to dance with and later escort some of the younger daughters to the family cars in the parking lot, but that was the limit of my party duty.

Occasionally, when there were two or three of my pupils from the same family, I was asked to drive out to their estate to give the lessons, as they all seemed to have their own tennis courts. The Club courts, I was proud to notice, were in better condition, and that was because they were brushed and rolled by me.

The room I was given was over the kitchen and next door to that of the golf instructor, a short, chunky Italian fellow, very friendly, who proposed that, whenever time permitted, we exchange lesson time; he showed me how to hit a golf ball and I did the same for him with tennis.

I did notice that nowhere during my summer experience did I ever encounter anyone with a Jewish name, or who appeared Jewish to me; but I did not dwell on that fact. Also, due to the absence of husbands during the week, I was aware that some of the lonelier young wives were being particularly attentive to me, so I went out of my way to be polite, but very proper. While I may have been tempted, I resisted.

The end of the summer approached, and I was busy arranging for the annual Club singles and doubles tournaments, getting some Prize Cups, etc. from Mike Blanchard, when Mr. Smith approached me to say that he and the Club president were pleased with my performance during the summer and wished to offer me the job for next year. I hastily accepted. He said that he would be phoning me sometime during October to work out the details. On behalf of the Club, he also invited me to attend their Labor Day Weekend functions, including the Saturday night dance, along with a date. I could also invite another friend and his date, all of whom would be guests of the Club and would be put up in rooms the Club maintained over its nearby garage. Extremely pleased, I sailed off to telephone Janet. The "other friend" would be my new roommate to be, John Ashton. I was pleased that the summer in Norfolk had turned out so well.

The Labor Day weekend was a great success. Janet and I were able for the first time to sleep together in the same bed for several nights—absent the Vassar 'one foot on the floor' rule: heavy petting, but no sex. We talked about classes, papers, professors, and a bit about after graduation plans. There was wonderful food throughout the weekend and a festive Labor Day dance with unlimited liquor by the Club. I then drove Janet to Vassar and back to New Haven I went. John was back in our rooms before I arrived. We talked about the great Labor Day weekend we both had enjoyed. His date had been a nurse from a local New Haven hospital, who hadn't seemed comfortable in the Club atmosphere or with our conversational interests. John kept telling me how attractive he thought Janet was—like I cared what he thought. But then the zinger came!

"I didn't know that Norfolk had changed its hiring policies" John said casually.

"What in blazes are you talking about?" I asked.

"Well, my parents have many friends who are members and we had been there as guests several times over the years, and knew that they never hired any Jews. When I asked Mr. Smith about it, he didn't seem to know you were Jewish."

"You asked Mr. Smith about me?"

"Well, I was curious," he stammered.

"You son of a bitch!" I shouted. "You went out of your way to make sure I was not hired back there, didn't you?"

"Not exactly, but it was of some interest to me and my parents."

I stood up and shook my finger in his face, screaming, "Now listen, you bigoted bastard! It's too late for me to get a different room now. But you see that bedroom on the left, that's yours and you stay there and keep away from me as much as possible. I'll certainly stay in mine as much as I can. And when I'm in the living room, with a girl or a friend, you stay in your bedroom or clear out completely, and I'll do the same for you. I want to see as little as possible of you while I'm stuck in these rooms!"

That's the way it went for a long while. He kept in his room and I kept in mine. When Janet came for a weekend dance, I kept the interchange with him to a minimum. Of course, John's inquiry about the Club's "change of policy" had done its task, and I never heard from Mr. Smith again.

When girls were present for weekend dances, the school permitted several entries in the Law Quadrangle to be emptied for the use of our female guests. The original tenants fended for themselves by doubling up on the sofas of friends or staying at the apartments of married classmates. Like others similarly situated, I had to stand watch over the nearby bathroom while my date used it, and later returned her to her women's dorm by early morning.

For many years I had been shy and unable to speak in public until a breakthrough came when I was somehow talked into participating in a Barristers Union mock criminal trial. My then roommate, John Ashton, toward whom I had some leftover bitterness, after he cost me the chance for a second summer as tennis instructor at Norfolk, had signed up to do one, an attempted rape case, and found a partner, who dropped out shortly after starting to work with him.

There were two law students on each side, the prosecutors and the defense counsel, of which John was one. Young students from the Yale Drama School played the witnesses. John was only my roommate because he had gotten control over a two-bedroom with a living room in between suite on the ground floor of the lower quadrangle and I wanted to escape from the single-room, dungeon-like garret where I had burned the midnight oil during our freshman year.

I shared some classes with a friend of John's from Bronxville, New York who opposed John as one of the prosecutors but John still didn't have a partner and the time for the start of the trial was fast approaching. One evening, Chuck and his partner descended on me in John's absence and begged me to sign up to partner with John as defense counsel. I was aghast and said, "Absolutely, no!"

I was incapable of speaking in front of a group, jury, judge, gallery or whatever. John waltzed into the suite about then, sniffed out what was going on, and immediately turned all his attention to getting me to relent and be his trial partner. He promised that the role would be primarily a minor one, as he had agreed with his first partner that he, John, would do all the hard work—the cross examination of the rape victim, the closing argument to the jury, and the evidence arguments to the judge. All I would have to do would be the opening to the jury—in essence, a short outline to what our case would be like, and then I could coast with only a short, unimportant witness or two. I resisted stubbornly that night and kept saying, "No."

For several days thereafter, John kept after me, explaining that I would mostly be sitting at counsel table as an observer, with he, doing all the objecting, arguing against the prosecuting team, and speaking to the judge and jury. When it was pointed out that if I didn't do all of them this favor, the case would have to be dropped, as with no partner for John, it could not comply with the requirement of four counsel, and none of them would get the trial experience they were seeking. Largely because of my friend Chuck, who by then had asked me to room with him our third year, I reluctantly and with great fear, agreed to try it, with the caveat that I reserved the right to cut my speeches on my feet to the bare minimum or to remain silent most of the time, relying on John to carry us through to what I thought was sure to be a bitter end. So, then for a couple of crowded days, John and I practiced our roles. I outlined the brief opening and mostly listened to John run through his cross of the drama student rape victim and his emotional speech to the jury. It sounded okay to me but what did I know.

The night of the trial finally arrived. Of all things, a large number of my friends turned up in the audience, together with many of the friends of the drama student witnesses, our opponent's friends and some family, as well as two faculty members. I decided to pay no attention to any of them and to just sit as quietly as I could through this terrible event. The trial eventually started. The judge, a real one invited from a court in New Haven, was pleasant and unthreatening. After Chuck's partner made his opening, which sounded good to me, I had to stand and do my opening. It didn't seem that difficult. After all, I had all but memorized most of the five-minute presentation and I sat down pleased with myself. I hadn't fainted and the jury seemed interested.

Then came the testimony of the trial itself. First and foremost, the rape victim, played by a most attractive and talented drama student, who had everyone on the edge of their seats, as one of our opponents led her through her story, with an incredible number of leading questions. That's when I realized trouble was brewing. No objections were coming from ol' John, who sat silent as improper question after question flowed from our opponent's mouth. I kept looking at him and whispering, "Object," at first quietly, then not so quietly. But from his face, I could see we were in real trouble. He was mostly pale white and looked for the first time to me, scared. I then realized that he was frozen in his seat and unable to even stand up. I whispered again, "What's wrong? He's almost finished. You have to do the cross! Are you all right?"

"No. No. You do it," came the answer.

I almost couldn't believe my ears. I looked over at Chuck who seemed to understand what had happened. He slid over a note scribbled on a piece of loose paper that read, "You do the cross. You know it by now. Good luck!" So, I had no choice.

The judge was getting annoyed after the prosecutor had finished, and nothing was happening. I stood up, heading to the lectern with my papers, politely introduced myself to the witness, then began asking some of the questions that I clearly remembered from John's practices. A couple of them were good and the witness had trouble with them. I became more confident and spoke clearly and slowly. Thereafter, I must confess that I don't remember a lot of the examination except to know that it felt good, and I knew that I had saved us from a disaster. Sitting down next to John, I whispered, "I didn't like what you did to me. Are you going to dump out on the closing also?"

"You better do that, too. I don't feel well. I can't talk."

He still had that frozen look on his face. So, that is what happened. I actually did the rest of the trial for our side; arguing against both opponents in front of the judge, and coming out on the better end of the battle. When it came to the closing to the jury, my blood was up and I was anxious to get at them. I got more confident as time went by and sat down with great satisfaction. I could see from some of the jurors' faces that they were impressed. God knows how it happened, but I guess it happened because there was no other choice and I did, indeed, have it in me. I finally found out! From that night on, I was a different person when it came to speaking in front of groups. I loved it and still do.

(I can't say that I owe my later career as a corporate trial lawyer to John, but I do believe something was building within me for many years and that practice trial was the catalyst that released my pent-up response to what had seemed like perpetual shyness. Never since has that been my problem. When I completed my first oral argument before the Supreme Court of the United States, I told my colleagues that it was an occasion when I thought back to my "Barristers Union" neophyte breakthrough with fondness.)

8

End of Second Year: My Summer at Birchwood Country Club

I was about to start applying to New York City law firms for the oncoming summer when I received a pleasant phone call from Mike Blanchard to arrange for my orders from Spalding for next summer. I had to tell him what Ashton had done and that I hadn't heard from Mr. Smith.

"Don't do anything rash yet, like apply to a law firm for one of their summer slave jobs. Give me a week and I'll be back to you," he said.

Sure enough, within a week, Mike called back to say that he had a marvelous deal set up for me at the Birchwood Country Club in Weston, Connecticut, a club composed almost entirely of extremely wealthy Jewish golfers, who had not the slightest interest in the two beautiful Hartru tennis courts on its grounds. He had made an interview appointment for me with the Tennis Committee of the Birchwood Club, none of whom knew anything about tennis.

"What do I tell them?" I asked.

"That you specialize in running Club tournaments for youngsters, so their fathers would be free to play golf. Here the trick is to do something to make sure the mothers stay off the golf course as well as the kids."

"No problem," I responded. "I'll deal with the mothers, award a lot of trophy cups, and give bargain-rate lessons to the ladies."

"You seem to have gotten the idea," laughed Mike and we agreed that I would call him right after the interview.

John, meanwhile, had broken an ankle skiing and his leg was in a cast, giving him much trouble walking. Sometimes, I agreed to carry his books if we were going in the same direction. But our friendship, such as it was, was over.

The interview with the Tennis Committee went even better than I could have imagined. I was dressed in my Ivy League best and met with a group of five well-dressed businessmen in a room bedecked with golf trophies and photos of former Club Golf Champions. Not one question was posed about my tennis skills or teaching experience. Blanchard, I figured, had done good preparatory work. The first question, by the Chairman, was: "What plans would you have to keep our wives and kids off the golf course?" Since I had driven down from New Haven to look over the Club and its courts two days earlier, I knew that many of the women sunned themselves in chaise lounges around the swimming pool during the mid-day hours.

"I would first visit the swimming pool area and distribute some of my flyers about the Special Rates for Group Lessons for the 9 to 12-year-old age group, as well as the even lower rates for the 13 to 16 year group, including free tournament entries and half-rate lessons for mothers." I explained. "I would have with me some of those silver and gold trophies I buy at specialty stores in Manhattan, and tell them that every pupil usually wins at least one."

The rest of the interview was a piece of cake. They loved me because I kept telling them that I would emancipate their golf course from the invading wives, daughters, mothers, etc. They explained that there was no room at the Club for me to use, but said there were reasonable single room rentals available in Weston or nearby Westport. The best news was that they had no interest in my tennis lesson income. Moreover, I was free to charge my lunches to the Club when I ate at the bar. Weston was much closer to Manhattan than Norfolk so whenever it rained (or looked like it might rain) I had my sign up that read "Courts Closed Due to Rain" and was off in my car to the City and Janet.

Mike Blanchard, by the way, went on to a fine career.

After being a Spalding salesman, he became a Referee at the Forest Hills Tennis Stadium, where the amateur championships were then played, and I chatted with him about old times when I attended matches. Then, when the new Stadium was built near Flushing Meadows he was put in charge of all officiating at the U. S. Open, the Davis and Wightman Cups, and other major tournaments (the Chief Umpire, I believe).

By the time my second academic year came to a close, I had become a Research Assistant to Professor Myres McDougal, due to my interest in public international law, and had written a chapter for his soon to be published treatise on that subject. It was on the subject of "Change of Circumstances" in public international law arbitrations. I had no idea how important that would become in my later career. I had also had my first Barrister's Union trial under my belt and was no longer shy about speaking in public.

The days and weeks at Birchwood flew by. My first day of work proved to be a success that lasted throughout my stay. I went to the pool area with my flyers, sample trophies and bargain lesson spiel for the heavily oiled ladies of the Club. They liked it and many signed up for their kids and themselves that day. I was always busy with either lessons or weekend and mid-week tournaments and handed out so many trophies that even I was embarrassed by the tactic. But everyone loved it. The two swimming instructors, Catholic boys from nearby St. Vincent's College, had my number and ribbed me endlessly about my tactics to which I retorted, "It's working, isn't it? So, you just keep laughing while I'm depositing some bucks in my almost-empty bank account."

Before the summer ended and I headed back for my third and final law school year, I was called home by my parents to help them with an extremely irritating family problem. I did so with alacrity for they had done nothing but sacrifice many things for my education and potential career. The problem related to a strip of some ten small stores located on a block called New Main Street in Flushing, where my parents still lived. In the real estate business, such stores were called "taxpayers".

My mother's successful real estate transactions had brought her into contact with Mr. Philip Godfrey, a local Long Island real estate tycoon, who owned the taxpayers, many other large real estate properties, as well as race horses, which he enjoyed entering in major stakes races at the Aqueduct Track on Long Island. She had offered to buy this strip of stores many times but had been rebuffed by Mr. Godfrey, politely each time. Some years earlier, he had finally relented when he purchased a major condominium development further out on the island; so my mother finally bought the taxpayers and my father, then retired, had become the manager of the stores, personally collecting the rentals on the first day of each month. While still an undergraduate at Michigan, I had kept the books for the stores and prepared the tax information for our accountant when home on spring, fall and summer vacations. The investment had been very profitable and my mother, who was concerned about the welfare of her aging parents, who had only recently sold their grocery store in The Bronx, decided to ensure their comfort by giving them one-half of the income from the stores. I, myself, often had the task of making out and mailing those rental income checks to my grandparents. We did not think it necessary to transfer the half ownership of the real estate to them, as we would always make sure they received their monthly income, which was all they cared about, and my parents paid all of the Federal and state income taxes on the property.

Then along came my mother's greedy sister and brother, each of whom had been total failures during their lives—my aunt having married a mostly out-of-work house painter, and my uncle, having only worked as a clerk in my grandfather's grocery store, and when it was sold, became unemployed. These two and their spouses now lived in New Jersey and connived to have their old parents live with one of them for six months at a time, in the process, stripping them of any monies or jewelry or assets of any kind, on the pretext of paying "something" for their rent. The old couple was getting senile, believed anything they heard, and soon it was all about how badly my mother, father and I were cheating them out of the property that they *owned* on New Main Street in Flushing. To counter this alleged cheating, they were encouraged to make out new wills that disinherited my mother entirely.

My parents did not care about being informally disinherited; they were furious at the dishonesty and lies that were being used to poison the minds of my mother's parents. For all the kindness, generosity, and love they had shown to these old people, it was hard to observe the situation with equanimity. I contacted Frank Guarino, my parents' real estate lawyer, who put me in touch with a good and reputable estates lawyer, who I retained for my parents. He wrote a firm, polite demand letter to my aunt and uncle, who were sufficiently terrified about being sued that they agreed to end their efforts at what the law terms "undue influence". I also took the trouble to drive out to New Jersey, meet with my grandparents with the books of the property, showing them that not only had they never been cheated, but that all of the income that they had been and would continue receiving had come from the total generosity of my parents, and particularly, their daughter. Moreover, they had never had to pay any Federal or state tax on this income. That appeared to take care of the problem, and I recall that not long thereafter, they both passed away, leaving virtually nothing in their estates.

Back to New Haven and my final law school year I went, knowing that one of my very real next problems was the impending end of my student deferment upon graduation, and my realistic prospect of being drafted into the Army for two years. Importantly, the shooting portion of the Korean War involvement by the United States ended with the Korean Armistice in 1953 under Eisenhower's presidency; but that would not prevent my being drafted for 24 months of service, if found physically fit.

The third year at most law schools is considered marginal and, in the view of many, unnecessary, other than serving as a money-producer for the school. As with many others, my third year became a jumble of disconnected activities. Some classmates were taking cram courses in order to pass the Connecticut Bar Examination so that they could apply for commissions in the Judge Advocate

General's Corps, but it was clear that such service added another year to one's active military service and so I passed that by. Apart from classes and research for Professor McDougal, I was editing what was then called the *Law School Newsletter*, but at the start of the Spring term, I spied a notice on the school bulletin board for volunteer interns at the U.S. Attorney's Office in Manhattan and called to inquire whether coming from New Haven would disqualify me. They put me in touch with a classmate who was also applying. I contacted him and the two of us were hired and arranged to travel into Manhattan every Wednesday evening, working at the Southern District U.S. Attorney Office on Thursdays, Fridays, and often on Saturday mornings.

The experience was not as exciting as my classmate, Marvin Segal, and I had hoped for. As we were from New Haven and the bulk of the other volunteer interns were from local New York City schools such as Columbia, NYU, and Fordham, they were able to capture the more interesting assignments by dint of being on the spot. Mostly this related to being assigned to a Criminal Division Assistant U. S. Attorney, who, of course, prosecuted criminal indictments and investigated possible new criminal charges, while the Civil Division Assistants defended U.S.

government agencies from suits for damages, for example, alleged damages from an accident involving a U.S. Postal Office truck.

Being late arrivals, we were both assigned to Civil Division assistants and spent more of our time in the Department library rather than sitting in on interviews with FBI agents or witnesses to alleged Federal crimes. My Civil Division Assistant could not have been nicer to me. He took me with him to Court every time he had to present an argument or appear before a District Judge or Magistrate, but the occasions were not numerous. At lunch, where the interns often traded tales with each other, Marvin and I had little of interest to offer in comparison to the stories from the criminal side.

At those lunches, the gossip often turned around which Assistant appeared to be the flavor of the day in the eyes of the head of the entire office, the United States Attorney for the Southern District of New York, at that time a Mr. Paul Williams, who had been appointed to that post by Herbert Brownell, Jr. Most of the time the name bandied about most of the time was "Dick Owen", allegedly Williams' fair-haired boy, who seemed to be given the pick of the criminal cases that drew newspaper attention. I did know a Yale Law graduate from the class of 1952 by the occasion of having sat in a small seminar on Legal Accounting with him, and as he had clerked for Judge Charles Clark on the Second Circuit bench after graduation, and now was a Special Assistant in the Criminal Division, I could get another and more knowledgeable viewpoint. His name was Martin Carmichael and he was unimpressed by the legal prowess of Dick Owen, and thought his reputation undeserved.

I simply tried to soak up as much knowledge as possible, and before I knew it, the internship was over. While it was on, Janet and I often arranged to see each other in Manhattan when my hours ended at noon on Saturday. She would be waiting for me at the Courthouse entrance, staying at her parent's apartment in The Bronx during these weekend visits. On one such occasion, I was invited to take her home and there met her mother, father, and younger brother, all of whom I liked and got along with very well.

My last weeks in New Haven were taken up by the minutiae of arranging with my then roommate, Hayden Ames, to try to sell all or most of our furniture to some undergraduates at the College or law students in the class behind us; in trying to invest my growing savings account moneys in some safe stocks for the two years of my anticipated Army service; and finishing up two longish papers for courses that accepted papers in place of a written exam; all boring but necessary tasks.

Graduation took place in May and I was pleased that my parents were able to attend and enjoy the ceremony, the speeches, and meet Professor McDougal, along with some of my friends.

9

Induction Into the United States Army

My three years of student deferments occurred during the shooting part of the Korean War. In 1954, when the war was over, the local draft board could no longer be denied, and I received a notice to take a physical exam on a Wednesday morning at the Whitehall Street medical facility on lower Broadway in Manhattan. I was still living in New Haven so I took the commuter train to Grand Central and then the subway and bus out to my parents' home in Flushing, where I slept overnight. My father had graciously agreed to my request to borrow his car for my next morning's trip into lower Manhattan for the physical.

Strangely, I was experiencing soreness in my knee and a slight redness around my left ankle, which also hurt when I put weight on it. This was the recurrence of a problem that I had encountered while in college, where the school doctors had concluded that I had a mild case of gout, which could be verified by occasional blood tests that would show an elevated level of uric acid in my body. What luck, I thought. At least I had some chance of failing the physical.

So I found a reasonable garage on a side street near the Whitehall medical facility, which had a special rate for a three-hour stay, exactly the length of time I had been informed would be required. There were hundreds of young men around my age in line for physicals that day. We chatted amiably as we waited, wondering about any chance of coming out with a 4F classification. I gathered that the odds were highly stacked against that result. As I proceeded from one doctor to another, having each part of my body checked by a different physician, there seemed little hope for a rejection. At last I saw the fellow in charge of legs, who did notice the redness and soreness around the knee and ankle and asked only if it hurt, to which I replied:

"Quite a bit!" He then scribbled a short paragraph onto my paperwork and told me to move on to the next doctor. When each of us was finished with the doctors, we were told to go to the Checkout Desk with our paperwork. As I waited in line in front of that last stop I observed that the white-coated official in charge had only two rubber stamps and an inkpad in front of him. Repeatedly, he slammed down the one, which left the large black notation "1A" on the papers of the potential draftee in front of him. Very rarely did he reach for the second stamp, which imprinted "4F" on the papers. As my turn approached, my apprehension grew and I wondered what the doctor had written about my leg. When the rubber-stamper had my

74

papers, he read the notes placed on them about my condition, pushed back his chair and opened a desk drawer in front of him, from which he withdrew a third stamp that none of us had seen before. He rolled it onto the stamp pad and with great firmness stamped my papers "For further observation—Governor's Island." I was told that they were sending me there straight away on a government bus.

"But what about my father's car? It's parked in a garage around the corner."

"That's your problem, son," the rubber-stamper quipped.

The best I could negotiate was access to a telephone, from which I made a collect call home, explained the situation to my father, read him the parking garage ticket and telephone number, so that he could call them and arrange a time when he could pick up the car after taking the subway into Manhattan. Shortly thereafter, I was on a bus to the ferry, which took me, along with several other potential inductees, to the hospital on Governor's Island on Wednesday late afternoon.

Depressing, it certainly was. There were five of us, placed in an isolation area, with sliding curtains separating us from sick Army soldiers. Several doctors stuck their heads in during the day on Thursday, but none looked at me. Of course, my ankle started hurting less as it usually did during the gout attacks. Did they know? Most of Friday dragged by, in total boredom; my only relief, a copy of the *Daily News* that I snatched from the desk of a hospital orderly. As one could predict, the doctor whose name was on my chart came in to examine me late on Friday afternoon. By then, there was no swelling or discoloration, and even I was not prepared to lie about my non-existent pain.

The doctor smirked at me and said, "These appear to be occasional episodes that you have and certainly not serious enough to prevent you from carrying a rifle."

I guess he thought he was amusing. I replied, "So, when I have one of these flare-ups while standing guard duty over some doctors' quarters in a combat situation, they'll have you to thank when I fail to perform properly."

"Clever one. I see from your file that you just finished law school. Makes sense. Good luck, Mr. 1-A."

I was released from Governors Island a 1-A, late on Friday, to make my way back to Manhattan and then to my parents for the weekend.

Back at school, a number of us who were now draft bait huddled together in a room in the Law Quadrangle, trying to figure out some scheme to improve our status. None of us were willing to spend the extra year in one of the military services in order to be an officer. For the Marines, it was a year and six months extra, and for the Navy, four years total. We decided to try the Army reserves through a local New Haven unit one of us had heard of that was supposedly desperate for volunteers. We selected Al Lerner, a tough CCNY graduate, with superb negotiating skills, to be our spokesman.

Al went to the Reserve Meeting one evening and came back saying that he made us a great deal. Only two reservists had shown up for the meeting and the Sergeant in charge needed to recruit some bodies or risk having the unit closed and being transferred away from New Haven, where he lived. So Al made a deal: the Reserve Unit would get all nine of us; we would have the Reserve rank of Corporal, which would remain with us if we volunteered for active duty upon receiving an induction notice; we would only have to attend every second weekly Reserve meeting; and we would not have to attend summer camp. We all agreed this probably was the best deal we could get so we each went to see the Sergeant and signed the papers to enlist in the Army Reserves. Needless to say, since we were all law students, we read the spots off the documents to make sure there was no extra year or any other catches.

After leaving New Haven in May, I moved to Manhattan to share a small apartment on Gramercy Park with the classmate who had been a volunteer intern with me in the office of the United States Attorney during our last semester of law school. A bed and a sofa bed, plus a small kitchenette served us adequately. I still had a serious attachment to Janet, with whom I spent most evenings, so all I needed was to study hard for the Bar Exam, take it, and then find some kind of temporary job to earn some money until the inevitable Induction Notice arrived in the mail. Inquiries at my local Selective Service Board only told me that my number would be coming up shortly.

I scoured *The New York Times* classified job ads, finally spotting as inconsequential a job advertisement as possible, since I knew it would be strictly temporary but I could not tell my employer that, for I would never be hired if they knew my actual status. The job was with the Prentice Hall State Tax Service, digesting Tax Court opinions for $65 a week, in a large room in an old building on lower Broadway. There was a time clock that I had to punch each day to make sure Prentice Hall got its pound of flesh.

Most of the employees were lawyers or law graduates from somewhere, happy for a job in the then current recession. The company representative in charge of the operation was a Germanic-looking, crew-cut wearing automaton, who had an empty desk at the back of the room observing each of us and making sure that we did not stop typing—ever! Never a smile, a good morning or good night, just a glare if someone was a minute late.

The Induction Notice arrived in late September, giving me ten days to get my affairs in order before reporting for induction at Whitehall Street again, in early October. I waited until the last Friday before my induction date so that I could collect my last paycheck.

That morning, my crew-cut boss stopped by my desk and snarled at me, "You know, Layton, a messy desk is a sign of a messy mind."

I shot back, "Well then, I assume you'd agree that an empty desk is the sign of an empty mind!"

His face turned red and he hurried away from me, stomping up the aisle.

At the end of that day, right before I punched out on the time clock for the last time, I went to his desk and said that, due to circumstances beyond my control, it was necessary for me to leave the employ of the Prentice Hall Corporation, and handed him my Induction Notice. He got the message, obviously realizing what I had been up to, and simply handed the paper back to me.

I had already been in touch with the Sergeant in Charge of my New Haven Reserve Unit, and arranged to volunteer for active duty as a corporal in the reserves a day or two prior to my arrival at Whitehall Street. There is a saying that "In the land of the blind, the one-eyed man is King," and that is the way I felt about being a corporal in the United States Army.

A military bus drove about 50 of us newly inducted captives to Fort Dix, New Jersey that early October morning. I was surprised at how cold and wet it was at the base. We were put in wooden barracks, given sheets to put on flimsy mattresses and one khaki army blanket, then told that all lights would be out at 9 o'clock. The following morning, a bugle went off at the ungodly hour of 5:30 a.m., followed by shouts of "Fall out, C Company!"

So, that's where I was. Lined up in the freezing cold, still dressed in civilian clothes, some Captain lecturing us unintelligibly in a twangy southern drawl. What I was able to understand was that we were going to be led by our Sergeants to the Mess Hall for breakfast, after which, the medics and dentists would have a look at us, and then the quartermaster would outfit us with uniforms, underwear, socks, belts, hats, fatigues, overcoat, etc. It was a busy day for all.

I survived my first Army meal, but not by much. I couldn't stand a lot of the food, so I settled for some bread, coffee and powdered scrambled eggs. When we reached the quartermaster's operation, I learned that while all of my companion GIs got serial numbers and metal dog tags that began with "US", mine began with "ER", meaning "Enlisted Reserve". That is how they knew to give me two V-shaped stripes to sew onto my military jacket, so all would know I was a corporal. They also made us sit down in a separate room and fill out something called a 201 Form, which asked a lot of questions about our education, special talents or interest, etc. Not knowing any better, I filled it out like I would an application to get into college, little realizing what impact that might have on my Army assignments. So here I was, 23 years old, a law school graduate and I was a corporal, a leader of men! The paradox was startling, but I had to try to carry it off.

Most of the young men in my company were from the hill country of Tennessee, and they took my corporal rank seriously. We got back from a day of shots at the Infirmary, then lectures on how to handle the M-1 rifle and such. A Sergeant assigned bunks to all the Privates and told me that, as a corporal, I had to move to the small room at the front of the barracks with its own door, light, and small table, directly across from his room down the hall. With reluctance, I stripped my sheets and blanket from the upper bunk I had been using in the large open area of the barracks and carried them to my new "Noncom's room". I felt sad leaving the young recruits from Tennessee, but they were supportive of my move and thought it was right because I had two stripes on my sleeve. They also told me with excitement that the dentist had yanked out most of their teeth as being rotten, and were preparing sets of false replacements, which might be ready by next week. I realized that not one of them had ever been to a dentist in his life and that this was a step up for them.

The next morning the Sergeant in the small room across from mine explained to me that he was part of the permanent 'cadre' who remained in this barracks continuously, in order to keep training the draftees who would follow us after we presumably graduated from our "First Eight Weeks" and went on to our "Second Eight Weeks" of more specialized training. The weather was cold and rainy, the roads muddy; we had to march from one destination to another in total silence, carrying our newly issued M-1 rifles, which we, as yet, had little idea how to use. We were told that there would be a list posted on our Company Bulletin Board about important information, such as who was assigned to KP each morning, and that we were responsible for checking the Board each day.

When we lined up each morning after the morning bugle call, usually in the cold, drizzling rain, a Sergeant called out our names and we had to respond "present" or sometimes a voice shouted "infirmary"; but I couldn't help noticing that whenever the name "DeRusso" was called out, there was no response and the Sergeant scribbled something on his clipboard. Some of the men whispered that he must be AWOL and in a lot of trouble.

"Sick call, anybody?" the Sergeant barked. A few hands went up and the men were told to "fall out" and wait by the side of the barracks to be lead to the Infirmary. I stood there in the cold morning wondering who this guy DeRusso was.

The days were long and boring. The *training*, if one could call it that, was pathetic. Usually there were not enough copies of the written manual materials for each recruit; the *instructor*, if one could use that word, appeared to know very little about his subject other than what he read from the written manual. Map Reading, Hand Signals, Squad Tactics, Calisthenics, Gas Mask Usage, how to clean and fire the M-1 rifle, were all given a cursory run–through, but I suspected that very little was retained by any of us since we were constantly cold, wet, muddy and anxious to get into a dry building as soon as possible. That didn't happen until about 4:30 p.m. each day, when we returned to our barracks and either just collapsed on our bunk, or waited in line for the showers, hoping the hot water would not run out before our turn. One evening on my return from a particularly muddy, cold and rainy outing, there was a knock on the door of my little room in the barracks.

"Come in," I said, and in came a short, very fat Private, whose uniform was completely dry though slovenly.

"So you're the Corporal who sloshes through the mud with these jerks every day? My name's DeRusso," he announced.

"So, where were you inducted?" I asked, thinking I would learn where he came from.

"I wasn't," he replied. "The FBI came after me in New Jersey where I'm from 'cause I never responded to any of their stupid draft notices; so they found me and dragged me over here. Those idiots wrote 'Involuntary Inductee' all over my papers. What are you Layton, a Voluntary Inductee? What a bunch of assholes all these schmucks are!"

"Who are you talking about?" I asked.

"All of them! That stupid black Captain who says he is the Company Commander and reads us those notices at

84

5:30 a.m. in the pourin' rain, the cadre Sergeants, those morons who run the Mess Hall, they're all dumb as hell. So, that's what I come to talk to you about. Are you going to keep playin' ball with them or will you try out my system for a day and see which is better?"

I was still puzzled so I asked him to explain.

He said, "The boys from Tennessee in the barracks told me you're almost a lawyer. Somehow, you're a corporal, and you seem like a nice guy and smart. So why the hell do you want to drag your ass around in the mud, the freezing cold and rain all day just because these idiots think it's a good idea?"

"Well, what else am I going to do?" I shrugged.

"Just come with me in the morning and follow what I do all day and then you tell me which scam is better. I'm not trying to force you to do anything, but I hate to see some guy with brains playing the game with all these knot heads."

"And what would I have to do?"

"At roll call, when they ask about sick call, you raise your hand and say you got a fever and chills. They'll tell you to fall out by the side of the orderly room and in a while someone will lead all the sick call men to the Infirmary. I'll be waiting for you there, and from then on, you just follow me."

"But who's going to lead the platoon during the day without me?" I naïvely asked.

"What's wrong with you? Don't people get shot, wounded, killed in this stupid Army and isn't there always some knot head stepping right in to take their place? What about that six-foot goon from Brooklyn I seen you jawing with some?"

"You're right," I remembered. "I did tell him that he could be Assistant Platoon Leader."

"So, that's it. He's your replacement! I'll see ya tomorrow mornin' at sick call and you'll see what I'm talkin' about," and with that, he waddled out of my room.

The next morning it was drizzling, but not badly, as we lined up in formation in front of our barracks. Roll call produced another "no-show" by DeRusso, and then came the call for Sick Call. I raised my hand and said, "Fever and chills." There were several gasps from among the Privates, and I asked the Assistant Platoon Leader to take over for me. He was obviously pleased and said he would do his very best. Murmurs of "Good luck, Corporal." and "Hope you get better," followed me as I headed for the side of the Orderly Room with the other "sick" men, to await being led to the Infirmary and my meeting with DeRusso.

DeRusso, who seemed to appear out of nowhere, was waiting with the sick call candidates from the other platoons and we trudged over to the Infirmary, where after a cursory examination by an Army nurse, I was given a "C" tablet and told to rest as much as possible during the day. "Standard GI bullshit," murmured DeRusso as he sidestepped the nurses. "They would've given you the same stupid pill if you said you had a broken leg. Now come on with me and let's get out of here."

I followed his shambling gait down a walkway toward a little building that I thought looked like the Officers Club.

"Wait! Where are you going? This is the Officers Club!"

"Exactly," he said. "Just keep quiet, follow me, and let me do all the talkin'."

Off we went, around the building corner and up a short staircase to a porch where a WAC Private set at an official looking desk with many lists in front of her.

"Kathy, this is my friend, Corporal Layton; he's here on the same set of orders as me so please sign him in with me for today. He'll probably be coming with me from now on, okay?" She smiled prettily, welcomed me to the Club, made out an index card for me, asked me to sign it, and wished me a nice day. I followed DeRusso through the door and into the Club, finding it hard to believe what I had witnessed.

"See?" DeRusso smirked. "Just like I said; piece o' cake. Speakin' of which, let's have a little something to eat. I'm starving."

He headed to a serving counter where plates of bagels, cakes, scones, crullers and oatmeal cookies were arrayed, followed by pitchers of hot coffee and tea. We helped ourselves to plates, cups and saucers and headed to a nearby table after DeRusso picked up *The New York Times*, *The Daily News*, and some Jersey City paper from a nearby rack. I hung my Army poncho over a nearby chair and couldn't believe where I was. First of all, I was warm and dry. I was certain we would be thrown out. In fact, officers were walking by and paying no attention to us. One or two, I couldn't believe, stopped to say "Hey, DeRusso. How you doin' this mornin'?"

"They all seem to know you here!" I blurted.

"That's right! I'm usually here every day for coffee and then lunch."

"You eat lunch here too?"

"Sure, and so will you."

"How do you do it? Who do they think you are? I don't get it!"

"No reason to go into all that now. Let's just have a good time today and see how you like it. We can go through the con some other time, that is, if you're interested in joining my club."

So, after a bagel and coffee for me and a chocolate cruller with a Coke for DeRusso, we leisurely read newspapers, until DeRusso said, "About time for lunch. Follow me."

He led me through a large double door into a dining room where each of many square tables with four seats and a glittery white tablecloth were arrayed with a small vase containing a single flower, plus napkins and silverware. A Private came over to us where we sat down having left our newspapers on the two empty chairs at our table. There were menus on the table detailing the fare for that day's lunch, and the Private asked politely what we would like. I listened as DeRusso ordered the clam chowder and a cheeseburger and fries; I opted for the soup and the club sandwich on toasted rye bread. "Amazing!" I managed to utter. "Don't we have to pay for all this food? In the mess hall, it's free."

"And that's what the food there is worth. Nothin'. But don't worry about the cost; they just put it on your monthly Officers Club bill."

"But I'm not an officer or a member here, so what do I do?"

"Remember that index card that Kathy had you sign?"

I nodded, still confused.

"Well, now you're a member! No sweat, man. Just enjoy."

So, we ate, then drank some coffee and had some dessert, and read the rest of our papers while officers ate at nearby tables and walked past our table, paying no attention to our non-officer status. Our lunch was leisurely, lasting until past 3 p.m., when DeRusso announced, "We should start heading back to the barracks before those assholes at that Company struggle back and try to take showers with our hot water."

I walked back with him, watched him strip down and proceed to take a long, hot shower. I took a very quick one, saying, "Don't you care if there's no hot water for the men who've been marching in the freezing rain all day?"

He just laughed. "You're a pisser, Corporal! Why should I care about those idiots? So what do you think about my day? We didn't have time to hit the PX or the Library, but we could do them tomorrow if you're game."

I had given the question some thought before he asked it and said, "No thanks, DeRusso. I appreciate your offer, but I just don't think I could live like that every day, while the men in the Company are sloshing through mud and rain and the stupid training exercises every day. I couldn't keep it up. Besides, I want to become a lawyer when I get discharged. I can't take the risk of being court-martialed or something like that. I appreciate your invitation and all but I'm going to have to go back to being with those kids from Tennessee."

DeRusso looked at me like I was crazy and said, "I thought you were a smart guy. Why hang out with all those morons and deadbeats? Think it over, and if you change your mind, just drop out for sick call again, and I'll pick you up. So long."

Off he waddled. I didn't see him for a long time—until the third week of our second eight weeks of basic—but when I did, it was a memorable incident that forever stays with me as proof of his cunning and craftiness, the consummate "involuntary inductee".

The remaining days of our first eight weeks were dismal: frigid, beset by constant heavy or drizzling rain. In the seventh week, I finally succumbed to a cold. I was terrified that I might get pneumonia, which guaranteed that you would be "recycled", that is, start the first eight weeks all over again.

Each Friday night was spent getting ready for "inspection" by the Company First Sergeant, whom the Captain would sometimes accompany. They used white gloves and when they ran a hand along the locker or shelf and smudges showed on the white glove, you received a "demerit", signifying ineligibility for a weekend pass, which were not given out until your eighth week anyway. Nevertheless, a lot of scrubbing and cleaning and neatening of footlockers took place on Friday nights, in terrorized anticipation of the Saturday morning inspections.

We headed into our eighth and last week being informed that we had to pass the Rifle Range Test or we would be recycled, and that the three men with the highest scores on the test would automatically get a Weekend Pass. My cold had worsened and I knew that I had a temperature by feeling my hot forehead; but the Infirmary was out of the question because no one trusted the Army doctors' ability to distinguish "pneumonia" from a broken finger, and being recycled was unthinkable. So, I decided to brazen the Test out, even though I was so sick that I could hardly see the targets on the 500-yard rifle range, let alone score well. It was still raining hard and very, very cold. I remembered DeRusso's offer, which seemed pretty attractive at the moment. I chose the more noble and suffering path and I had to think of something quick. I had to think like DeRusso.

I inquired amongst the more knowledgeable wise guys in my platoon to see if anybody knew of a scam to pass the test. I found out that a Private in the Company, down in the dugout area below the targets, who had the job of target pulling and noting the score after each shot fired, was offering his talents with an M-1 pencil for $10 a test. Freely translated, that meant if I slipped a $10 bill to this wise guy in my company, he would arrange with someone named Sprizzo in Company F for me to have a pencil jam the bull's-eye—or very near it—on many of my shots so that I could get a passing or higher score. I gladly forked over the $10 bill, to be split I assumed, between Sprizzo and my wise guy, and awaited my turn at the test range in the pouring rain, feeling faint from my cold and temperature.

Finally, my turn came. We were all required to fire from a prone position, with legs spread out behind us, after our assignment target was raised up. I had been informed which target was being "pulled" by Sprizzo and I had easily arranged to shoot at that target. On my first two or three shots, I tried hard for the bull's-eye but had no idea how well or poorly I did, as there was rain on my glasses and my eyesight was affected by my cold and shivering.

Fortunately, there was walkie-talkie communication between the target caller and me. The set squawked and I heard a voice—undoubtedly Sprizzo's—shouting, "Tell that asshole to miss the target completely! He's fucking everything up by hitting the blank space away from the target and there will be too many holes on the target if he keeps this up."

So, I aimed high above the target, and heard him shout, "That's better! Keep it up!"

Then, all of a sudden, I felt a kick in my rear by the hard boot of the rifle range Sergeant, who was patrolling the area behind the shooters.

"Where the hell are you aiming, son? At the moon? Lower that rifle and try to hit the target!"

"Yes, Sergeant, I will," I mumbled.

I just stopped shooting until I saw him move down the line to yell at someone else, and then resumed aiming at a nearby hill, until I heard Sprizzo say, "Okay, that's enough. I think I got you passed." He meant, of course, that he jammed his pencil through either the bull's-eye or first ring enough times to score enough M-1 pencil points for me to pass. I stood up and headed back to the Company truck, barely able to clamber aboard over the back gate and slumped down into an almost immediate fevered sleep.

Back at the barracks, since it was Friday night, I cleaned my small room as best I could and then crawled into bed without even thinking of going to the mess hall. I fell into a deep sleep and awoke to Saturday morning's bugle call feeling slightly better. I felt much, much better when, standing at roll call with the rest of the Company, I heard the Captain read off the names of the men who had scored highest on the Rifle Range Test and heard my name read as third-highest in the company, thus qualifying for a weekend pass!

Hard to believe, but I was packed and out of there headed for the bus stop so fast you would've never thought I'd been teetering towards pneumonia. I used a pay phone while waiting at the bus stop to call my mother collect, telling her I was on my way home for the rest of the weekend and to please make an emergency appointment for me with the family doctor or else I was headed for pneumonia and a second eight weeks of this madness. She said she would do so immediately and was looking forward to seeing me. I arrived at the Port Authority Bus Terminal, took the subway out to Flushing, and a cab to my parents' house. After driving me to a new doctor, who was much better than the incompetent who had been the choice of my mother's circle of canasta players, I learned I didn't have pneumonia. He gave me some pills, told me to drink hot soup, tea, no solids, sleep a lot, and I could return to Fort Dix on Sunday night with no fear of pneumonia. I followed the directions precisely and headed back to Fort Dix by bus, arriving 15 minutes before my pass ran out on Sunday night. Another good night of sleep helped, and I woke to be informed that everyone in the barracks has made it past the first eight weeks and we were to wait in the mess hall after breakfast to learn of our Second Eight Weeks assignments.

I was hopeful that a fuss I had made one day at the eye clinic would pay off for me. I complained to an eye doctor about my vision, saying that my astigmatism was worse than my glasses corrected for.

"Listen, Doctor," I pleaded, "All I need is for you to write 'Restricted' on my 201 File and they can't put me in the Infantry!"

"Why should I do that, son?"

"Because I'm Jewish and so are you," I replied.

He said he didn't care for thinking like that but then agreed and said, "If this is that important for you, okay, I'll do it. But you realize it still might not work."

"I know, but I'll take my chances," I said. That morning, I was assigned with many others, to our second eight weeks of training at Fort Dix Clerk/Typist School, exactly what I had been hoping for.

We were moved to different and better barracks for Clerk-Typist School and a First Sergeant, after looking us over and noticing my corporal's stripes said to us, "This fellow with the two stripes is going to be the Class Leader of this class at the School."

I reminded myself, *'In the land of the blind, the one-eyed man is King.'*

Turning to me, he said, "You have to pick your own Squad Leaders by electing them or the Class Leader just appoints them."

By this time, I had caught on to the Army's ways enough to recognize that nepotism was going to be my best way forward, so I said quickly, "I'll appoint them after we have a little discussion. So, you guys who were in my old barracks—I'm willing to appoint you if you understand my rules. Everything I say, you do; otherwise, no weekend pass. I always get a weekend pass and no KP."

Five hands went up to accept my appointments. "We need three more Squad Leaders willing to live up to my rules. Any takers?" More than three hands shot up, so I picked them by a quick look and a hasty judgment.

"You, you and you," I pointed. "If you step out of line with me, you'll be replaced immediately, along with pulling a day of KP. Do we understand each other?"

"You bet, Corporal," came the chorus of answers. So now I knew that my Second Eight Weeks were going to be a piece of cake, my only problem being how to figure out learning to type without looking at the keyboard and not dying of boredom.

My first query as Class Leader came from a saxophone player who wanted to investigate why he didn't pass the test for playing in the Fort Dix Band, when he came up to me and asked for permission to visit Battalion Personnel, which was what I had suggested he do; so, I signed a 2-hour pass for him to do that. He returned about an hour later looking very puzzled. He told me they let him look through all the applications and tests for the Band, and when he found what he was sure were his papers, his name had been crudely crossed out, and in its place, also crudely written in was the name "Private DeRusso, C Company". He said the clerks could do nothing for him, and he left me scratching his head and mumbling to himself.

Not many days later, our Class was enjoying a half-hour break at the Base PX and heard the noise of a band coming down the main street of the Battalion. A large banner was draped across the front of the marchers that read "Fort Dix Marching Band" and some 30 musicians were rendering

"The Stars and Stripes Forever" pretty much in tune, each member lustily playing his instrument; all, that is, except for one, whom I immediately recognized at the rear of the column. He was out of step, fat, and in disheveled uniform, as usual, dragging a saxophone by its mouthpiece, most of the instrument bumping along on the dirt street. It was none other than DeRusso, who spotted me, smiled and waved, and pretty soon was gone, following the remainder of the Band making a left turn out of my sight. That was the last I ever saw or heard of him. Many, many years have passed since 1954 at Fort Dix and I strongly suspect that he did not die a peaceful death in bed.

The remainder of my time at Clerk/Typist School was largely uneventful. My handpicked Squad Leaders did most of the administrative tasks and I read and rested to my heart's content except for worrying about the assignment I would get as a Clerk/Typist somewhere in one of the Army's global outposts. Rumors were flying about the place, based on some of the assignments of the prior Class after their 'graduation', i.e. Spain, Germany, France, Belgium; Baltimore, Washington, D.C. None of these sounded bad, but I had a strong preference for remaining stateside because of my girlfriend and the possibility of seeing her occasionally when I earned some leave. So,

Baltimore and D.C. were at the top of my wish list.

As much as I had learned about tampering with the Army's bureaucracy from my adventures with DeRusso, I was still reluctant to attempt to intrude into the assignment bureaucracy, always due to fear of being court-martialed if caught, and thus, be unable to pass the Character Committee requirements for Admission to the New York bar. I had no alternative but to await the day of our so-called 'graduation' from Clerk's school, to learn what the Army's grab bag had produced.

While still at Fort Dix, I bumped into one of my group of nine classmates who had become Corporals through the New Haven reserve unit, and learned that Lerner had been sent to Germany, and Baronoff and Gladstone to France. I didn't think my stateside chances were good, as I was also a Corporal, if that figured in any way in the Army's thinking. The day finally arrived, and the Sergeant started reading out our names alphabetically: Spain, France, Germany, Texas, California, Baltimore, were all being called out, with various wisecracks being shouted out while nervous eyes stared at the Sergeant and his clipboard. Finally, "Layton, Robert, Corporal: Special Assignment."

One of the men, noticing my stunned expression, reassured me, saying, "Don't worry Corporal. That's probably the Pentagon or the Judge Advocate's department 'cause you're almost a lawyer."

"Wow!" came the responses from the others. "Maybe it's in the White House or somethin' really special."

I waited till all the rest of the assignments were read out. None were like mine. I asked the Sergeant what I could do to find out what it meant. He was very helpful, saying he had not heard that kind of assignment before, so suggested I go down to Battalion personnel after lunch and ask them what it meant. I thanked him and followed his suggestion. Of course, the incident with the Fort Dix band came rapidly to mind, but I shrugged that thought away.

Right after the mess hall, I strode down to the Personnel Office in Battalion Headquarters. There I found two Privates, one more officious than the other, each claiming that he had no idea what this particular Special Assignment was, and that I should wait while they looked it up. After scrambling through some files they looked at each other and one said "JTF Seven", like that somehow made everything clear.

"Listen, you wise guys! No more game playing! Where the hell am I being sent?" I said, raising my voice, since I did outrank each of them.

"Well, JTF Seven stands for Joint Task Force Seven.

That is located on Eniwetok Atoll in the Marshall Islands. Since you probably don't know where that is, in the corner of the office over there," he began, pointing to the other side of the room, "is a globe Atlas that spins around. I think it's somewhere between Hawaii and the Philippines." So I looked, spun, looked closer and finally found a speck on the globe labeled "Marshalls" and one of the tiny islands said "Eniwetok". "What in the world is the Army doing there?" I asked. One of the two wise guys said: "Don't know about the others, but you're going out there to run the Island's newspaper—it's called *The Atomic Times* 'cause they tested the atom bomb there and they're gonna test the hydrogen bomb while you're there. It's one page and you'll have two Privates under you to do the donkey work."

"How did you two geniuses decide that I was the guy to send out on this assignment?" I asked.

"Well the truth is the slot requires a rank of Corporal and when we read your 201 File and saw you were on your college newspaper and an English major, it seemed a cinch decision. We didn't pay much attention to the location."

"But I put that stuff on my 201 File because I thought it would help me get a soft job in DC or the Pentagon, not stuck out in the middle of the Pacific on a coral atoll."

"Well, that's the breaks. The guy you're replacing made

it through 12 months there and so will you."

"I don't know how I'll ever be able to thank you two enough, but don't go out alone at night while I'm still around here," I warned. I could've killed those wise guys!

"It's only a year assignment. Army regs won't allow anyone to stay any longer."

"Can't thank you birds enough, but how about switching me to someplace in the States?"

"Sorry but it's too late. We'd never find anyone as qualified as you. The year will just whizz by."

So that is how I came to be the Editor of *The Atomic Times*—somewhat unbelievable, but true.

10

Life on the Island

My travel orders provided for flights on civilian aircraft to San Francisco and then to Honolulu, Hawaii, but the final leg was on a military cargo plane that could not have been more uncomfortable. As we circled the Atoll prior to landing I peered out my window and saw that there were no trees in sight, just glaring white coral, which triggered in my memory a chat I had with a grizzled Regular Army Sergeant at Dix before leaving, when I learned that he had completed a one-year tour on Eniwetok. He had quipped with a smirk, "You'll love it. There's a beautiful native girl behind every tree." So looking at the barren atoll, I realized how naïve it was to pay any attention to anything said by a Regular Army veteran.

Loud jeers greeted us as we disembarked down the stairs from the plane. "Whitemeat, whitemeat!" The *old-timers* shouted, lined up outside the flimsy airport passenger area, deeply tanned, wearing khaki shorts and brightly colored Hawaiian shirts; the off-duty island uniform, I quickly learned.

Comments such as, "If I had twelve months to serve on this Rock, I'd shoot myself", were one of the kinder epithets hurled by our welcoming committee.

"Hunnert and twenty-two, that's all I have left."

He was answered by "If I had that much time left on this hell-hole, I'd slit my throat."

Obviously, riding down to jeer at the new monthly arrivals was one of the Island's few entertainments, and I looked forward to the day that one of these uncomfortable military airplanes provided my exit on the way back to Honolulu and later, my eventual discharge.

So, off to our housing we were taken in a tiny bus, dropping some at Quonset huts and some at tents, one of which was my home for the next 12 months. I was assigned to Headquarters Company, logical because I was both a Clerk/Typist and *The Atomic Times* honcho. Our Headquarters Company First Sergeant made clear that our duties began at reveille (6 a.m.) and ended at lunchtime, so that there was nothing to do in the afternoon other than amusing oneself. Morning uniform was khaki short-sleeved shirts, with rank insignia, if any, sewn on by each soldier, and the famed khaki shorts, with khaki socks, plus an overseas cap for when we were outdoors.

The weather was the same every day—bright sunshine, only occasionally interrupted by a brief rain shower, almost never lasting more than two or three minutes. In the evening, however, we were occasionally hit with a heavy downpour that caused many of us to leave the outdoor movie; others watched in the rain wearing their ponchos and safari rain hats.

For me, each day began by donning my uniform: short-sleeved Army shirt bearing my rank insignia. By this time the U.S. Army had changed some of its rank nomenclature, one being that I was no longer a Corporal but a Specialist 3rd Class (SP 3), designed to distinguish between staff personnel and infantrymen—Corporals, Sergeants, Sergeant Majors, etc. Mostly, a lot of nonsense, but I had to sew an SP 3 insignia on my shirtsleeve just the same. Some months later, I was actually promoted to SP 2 (formerly, a Sergeant) not because I had done anything to deserve a promotion, but based on the Army's most standard promotion criteria—time in grade, that is, staying alive and not being court-martialed. Thereafter, a short visit to the mess hall for some very bad food, which one eventually got used to pushing around on a plate and eating some of it on occasion. The waffles or pancakes were bearable.

Then, I was off to the office of *The Atomic Times* where the two Privates who constituted the "staff" would stroll in at their leisure and then try to find some articles on the Associated Press teletype machine—which some clever

Army technician had been able to arrange for us to intercept on most days, and thus copy their news coverage for our captive readers. Most of the island's inmates cared little about the articles the Privates copied from the AP wire; they only cared about and read the sports stories; both baseball and football in those days. Nothing fancy like soccer or ice hockey then interested the American male population. My first major management crisis came when the boys (Private Miller, a graduate of the University of Illinois and Private Harris, recently of Brown University) told me that the connection to the AP wire had been lost for several days and they didn't know what the game scores were or even which team had won. I solved this major crisis in the following clever manner:

"Boys," I began, "Just wait a day or so until we get connected to the AP again; then we'll work with the Team Standings column. That way, we'll be able to figure out how many games had been played since our last story. Then, let's say the Yankees are our interest, we could know how many games the Yankees won or lost since our last story."

Of course, we could not know the scores of the missing games or what happened in the game, but who cared. I told them to have some fun and write the missing games up from their own imagination—as long as the winning and losing stats matched up with the new standings that we would soon be able to read. They were delighted, had some fun doing the writing. Even I wrote up a game or two—and our readership was none the wiser, but pleased to know who was ahead in the several pennant races.

The next problem arose when Private Harris came to me and said he would like to write a movie review column for the paper.

"What in blazes for?" I blurted. "No one cares whether the movie is good or bad!"

We only had one movie each night and the worst of it was that the T & E (Training and Education) people only circulated 60 movies throughout all of the Pacific atolls, so we were doomed to see each of them close to six times each before a man finished his one year tour. Harris, who was somewhat effeminate, wore blue sneakers and smoked Kool cigarettes, responded that he knew that but wanted the writing practice and to preview the movie for his review in the air-conditioned room where the film camera was located. I responded that I would ask for permission from the Major in charge of this area, but if he said "No", that was the end. So I went to Major Murphy, a West Point graduate who was intelligent but slightly delusional. He was convinced the Russians were planning to invade Eniwetok to prevent the Hydrogen bomb testing from taking place.

His response was "Let him give it a try, but I generally think it's a waste of time."

So, Harris started his reviewing and, of course, pretty soon there was a major problem. Harris wrote a review of an ordinary Chicago gang mobster movie and panned the blazes out of it. His review was sarcastic, damning in every conceivable way and concluded by saying that, in the reviewer's opinion, it was one of the worst movies ever made. I never screened his reviews because I was too lazy and bored; but after reading it as printed, I was waiting for Murphy to strike. I didn't have to wait long.

I was soon hauled before the Major, standing at strict attention as he barked, "What is wrong with this idiot Private? Doesn't he realize that the morale of these men is our concern? And what are they to do? Because he thinks it's a bad movie, they shouldn't go to see it? There is no other movie. This was a stupid idea in the first place, Layton. I blame you. Tell Harris the movie reviews are cancelled, and to get back to his regular work."

But I was far from through with Major Murphy. Several weeks later I was again hauled before him, awakened from a sound early afternoon nap by a runner who informed me that the Major had just read the day's edition of *The Atomic Times*, was quite upset and wanted me in his office immediately, meanwhile muttering about court-martial offenses under his breath. I stood at rigid attention when he handed me a copy of that day's edition that had several words in the lead story heavily circled in red crayon. "What is the meaning of this, Layton?" I scanned the story quickly, and replied:

"Those words do contain typos, for which we do apologize but that often happens in newspaper work, Major."

"Not under my command!" he shouted. "Now listen here carefully, Specialist Layton. I am going to give you a direct order. There will be *no more* typos in *The Atomic Times* stories. And if they do appear again, you will be court-martialed for disobeying a direct order."

"But Major," I tried to explain. "Typos are inevitable in a newspaper on occasion!"

"Nonsense!" He shot back. "It's your job to proofread this paper before it goes to press, so I'm holding you responsible. No more typos—understood?"

"Yes, Sir," I dejectedly replied.

And so it went. I trudged back to the office and

proceeded to unload on Harris and Miller.

"I'm not going to be court-martialed because of you two slobs. Read every story twice before you bring that rag of a mimeographed sheet to me each morning so I can now proof it with a magnifying glass and a dictionary. But I'm damned if I'm going to risk my bar admission because of you two meatheads."

Things quieted down for several weeks during which not one typo was uncovered. But then I found myself standing at strict attention one afternoon once again before Murphy, this time with the entire lead article of the mimeographed sheet circled by his infamous red crayon lines.

"What is the meaning of this, Layton?" I didn't get it right off, as there were no typos. It was a story about a regular Army First Sergeant who had been reported as 'missing in action' in the Korean War and wasn't heard from for several years. In the interim, his wife had decided that he was more than likely dead, and had managed to get herself remarried. He then was released by the Koreans, came home to find another man living in his house with his wife and children.

"What are you trying to do Layton, undermine the morale of the troops on this island? Have you no common sense? What was the need to reprint that terrible story? From now on if you have any question about how an article might affect morale, ask me. Do you understand?'

"Yes, Sir," I snapped, happy that there were no threats of another court martial.

And so it went; one idiocy after another as my weeks were passing by, albeit slowly. The painful irony was the fact that editing this rag was the reason I was chosen to live on this coral prison for a year.

11

Passover in Hawaii

I had arrived in late November 1954. I had been told
that an Army regulation specified that no personnel could
be stationed on Eniwetok for longer than one year. I learned
that it was strictly enforced. It also said that each EM
(enlisted man) was entitled to one week of R&R (Rest and
Recuperation) during his tour. Most men, I discovered,
saved their R&R for late in their tour and opted for Japan as
the locale since it had recently become available and stories
that were carried back by early adventurers raved about
both the beauty and availability of Japanese women. So, I
began to do research in the regulations and came across a
little known proviso for something called a "Religious
Retreat" which stated that every EM was entitled to attend
services conducted by a person trained in his or her religion
during important religious holidays. It was then
approaching April when the Jewish holy days of Passover
took place. I knew from working occasionally as a clerk in
the Headquarters Company Office that there were only a
Protestant and a Catholic Chaplain on the Island; not
enough Jewish personnel for a Jewish Chaplain, I guessed.
I investigated and found that there were a grand total of

eight Jewish enlisted men, and one Air Force Lieutenant, who was due to leave in the midst of Passover. I knew most of the eight enlisted men and so I called them to a meeting in the paper's offices one night.

There I explained my plan to them. I would prepare an official request on behalf of the eight of us to attend Passover services in Honolulu where I was certain a temple as well as a Jewish Chaplain could be found. I told them that in order for this to work it was essential that we all stick together, let no one else know what we were up to, and that they must agree that I would be our leader, making all decisions. I outranked them, in any case.

Right off the bat, one of them said, "What about that Jewish Air Force officer; he claims to have led the High Holiday services last year?"

"Leave Lt. Hoffman to me," I said. "He got me to help him build a tennis court on the air strip last December. He owes me and I can get him to remember how little he knows about Passover very easily. Besides he rotates in the middle of Passover."

So I wrote the memo very carefully and simply to the Island Commander, explaining that we were entitled to a Religious Retreat—according to the Army—under these circumstances, and that the closest Temple/Jewish Chaplain was in Honolulu. The Island Commander was a Colonel and a West Point graduate, who asked me to come to his office after I had submitted the request Memorandum through proper channels. When I stood at attention before him, he told me to relax and be at ease. He complimented me on my cleverness in locating this regulation and using it to such advantage. When I heard this, I could not help but think back to my adventures with DeRusso and thought that he might approve of my clever scheme.

The Colonel said to me, "I think you got us, Layton. I might have to approve your request. But then, there is the other partner who has to agree: the Jewish Chaplain in Honolulu. I will notify you of any response. Dismissed."

I did not have to wait more than two or three days before I was summoned back to the Colonel's office.

"We have a reply from Honolulu, from a Captain Hirsch, who is the Jewish Chaplain for Hawaii, Layton, and I suspect you won't much care for it."

He handed me a TWIX (a telex used by the armed forces) addressed to himself which basically said that rather than trouble eight soldiers to have to travel to Honolulu, he was prepared to send his assistant rabbi, a Lt. Schwartz, to our island to conduct our Passover services, and hoped this would solve the problem outlined in the Colonel's TWIX.

"Nice try, Layton," said the Colonel, "but I think you've been checkmated."

I returned to the tents where most of my Seder-needy Privates lived and called a meeting.

"This is where we need some Jewish ingenuity," I said. "Which one of you has parents or relatives that live in Los Angeles or thereabouts?" I asked. One hand shot up. "I do," said Private Harold Horowitz. "My folks live in Beverly Hills and they would have flown to Honolulu to see me if we had gone there."

"I gather that money is not a problem for them," I suggested.

"That's right. My dad's a Hollywood agent and represents a lot of movie stars. He and my mother are worried about my being on this Island when the tests start."

"OK. Now I have an idea. Let's you and I make a collect phone call to him tonight and ask him to explain life to that idiot Captain Hirsch, as one Jew to another, and your father must be a pretty smart talker to start with if he's a successful agent. Hirsch has to understand that we want to come to his Seder services and not stay on the island," I explained.

"You're on!" said Harold. "I've called them before, and anyway, my Mom loves to hear my voice."

It didn't take Harold's father more than ten seconds to see what we were up to and what we wanted him to do. He promised to have a very basic heart-to-heart conversation with the dear chaplain; and then we just had to wait.

Several days later the Colonel sent for me again.

"I don't know what you've been up to Layton but that Honolulu Chaplain of yours seems to have had a change of mind. Read this."

He handed me another TWIX from Hirsch stating that unexpected emergency problems prevented his assistant rabbi from leaving Honolulu, and so it would be necessary for the eight of us to fly to Honolulu! He recited the fact that he had now made arrangements for each of us to stay in the homes of individual members of his congregation, and would look forward to greeting us at the military airport on our arrival. I was able to keep a straight face before the Colonel but when I was plenty far from his office, I ran with glee to tell the others that Harold's father had scored a home run, and we would be getting off the Island for some days in Honolulu!

I had neglected to tell my boys not to tell anyone else about our expected "religious retreat" and the result was a fair amount of resentment toward us from our Catholic and Protestant island dwellers. "Leave it to the Jews to find some angle" or words to that effect, they would hurl at us whenever they saw us together. But, so what? Who cared? We were going! Then we were told we would be on next Thursday's flight to Hawaii, how much carry-on stuff we would be allowed, and that we were expected back some eight days later. The day finally came and we withstood the catcalls from the tent barracks as we loaded onto several jeeps for the ride to the airstrip. The C-47 transport was pretty uncomfortable, with only hard metal seats, cramped in among a large number of Stateside-bound mailbags. We didn't care.

Not long into the flight, the pilot's voice came on over the speaker system to inform us that there appeared to be a problem with one of the engines, and that if he couldn't get it fixed before we passed the point of no return (exactly halfway to our destination) he would have no choice but to return to Eniwetok to have the problem remedied. What a let down! Of course, that's what happened. We turned around and several hours later were back on The Rock, as some wags had named our island prison. The trip back to our Quonset huts featured delighted jeers and barbs from the Catholic/Protestant well-wishers, and we tried hard to ignore them and to pass the time while mechanics worked on the plane's problem engine. Our orders were to stick together, for once the replacement part was installed, the crew did not want to have to go looking for any of us; we were to be in one group. So, we decided that Monopoly was the simplest game to keep our minds occupied and that is what we played, for the six hours it took for the repair.

Finally, in the air again, I thought it best to give the group some instructions on how to behave after we landed. I explained that until we reported to Chaplain Hirsch, I was in charge of them. Thereafter, they were on their own, getting as much out of the available religious fare as they felt they needed. I reminded all of them as to the date and time of our return flight which was imprinted in bold lettering on our orders (you don't travel anywhere in the Army without typed orders) and, of course, the theory was that if you missed a flight, that was disobeying an order, and naturally, a court-martial offense. By this time, I was somewhat skeptical about the Army's enforcement system. I had arranged with Private Arnold Stahl, a member of the group with whom I had become somewhat friendly, that we would try to stick together on this Honolulu venture. On landing, we were effusively greeted by Captain Hirsch, who had a copy of our orders and a clipboard from which he began reading a list of our names, each paired together with a family from his congregation with which we would be staying. He seemed very pleased that he had been able to match up a family for each one of us, and beamed when he announced that I, the leader of the pack, would be staying at the home of Chaplain and Mrs. Hirsch. He was also reciting the times of certain services in the local temple, when I interrupted and pointed out that we had had a long flight and would welcome washing up, if he did not mind.

"Certainly," he responded. "There is a military latrine next to those hangars on your right some 500 yards away."

"Thank you very much, Chaplain. Private Stahl and I will rejoin you shortly."

Stahl and I headed for the hangars, but then spotted what we were really looking for—an Avis Rent-A-Car office—raced over to it, and proceeded to rent a nice looking convertible for at least one week, roared out of the air strip and onto the highway leading to Waikiki Beach, as fast as we could safely drive, never in our lives to see Chaplain Hirsch again!

We checked into the Waikiki Biltmore, after looking over all the other available luxury hotels, largely because most of its rooms surrounded a gorgeous designer swimming pool and the rooms had small terraces looking down onto the pool. Cost was not a problem as we were stuffed with our Army pay, which we couldn't spend on

The Rock. So we slept, ate, and drank martinis, roamed the streets and hotel lobbies hoping to pick up some local girls, but our Aloha shirts and khaki shorts were no match for the Navy and Air Force competition we faced, so we spent a lot of time poolside, chatting up the hotel waitresses. Any kind of female company is what we missed. We did keep track of the days and sooner than we liked, became aware that we had to return the car rental and report to the airstrip for our return flight to our island paradise. We did so sadly and had to listen to some boring tales on the flight back from the few who actually attended Seder and temple services. The next morning, I was directed to appear before the Colonel again and was prepared for the worst. He handed me the TWIX he had received from Captain Hirsch, which described with great annoyance the fact that Stahl and I, and a couple of others, had failed to show up for any religious activities, along with the suggestion that some form of company punishment might be appropriate. The Colonel asked me if it was true, which I readily acknowledged, and then asked me what I thought might be an appropriate punishment. While I was pondering that one, he reached over to take back the TWIX from me, and with a big smile on his face, tore it up into several pieces.

"You are dismissed, Layton. Go back to your duties and

try to finish out your tour on the Island without getting into any more episodes like this one."

I didn't ever see him again as his rotation date was not far off, but I always remembered him as someone who made a career in the military appear to be, on occasion, a class act.

12

Back on The Rock

Since isolation and lack of female company were aspects of life on The Rock that made survival difficult for those with limited interests, the Army had a Regulation that required a military I.Q. Equivalency Score of at least 100 in order for any enlisted man to be assigned here. Unfortunately, this Regulation was often honored in its breach as I discovered when I occasionally was transferred temporarily to be a clerk in the Island Commanders Office. There, I saw the 201 Files of all newly arrived personnel and was upset when I saw how many newly arriving men had Army I.Q. Scores in the eighties and low nineties.

"What happens to these guys?" I asked.

A Sergeant Major answered me by saying that sometimes some men drank so much they were hospitalized and sent back to the States to be dried out, some deliberately engaged in sex with other men to get caught, knowing that was conduct that could get them court-martialed. They were tried, convicted and flown off the island for a term in the stockade. When I asked why they were allowed to stay with under 100 scores, only a shrug of the shoulders was the response. It seemed that the only thing the Army could get right was the one-year limit on the tour of duty on Eniwetok.

The results that the loneliness and boredom brought about were reflected in the excessive drinking that took place each night either after or during the outdoor movies we saw. It was commonplace for the MPs to be seen dumping the drunken bodies out of wheelbarrows onto the ground in front of tents or barracks at the end of many evenings.

Men like me, who had been to college, used the library a great deal, wrote lots of letters to friends and family, and even tried to get some writing published. In addition to reading a lot, I played chess by mail with Janet, went swimming and water-skiing many afternoons, had a Monopoly game between dinner time and the start of the evening movie, and every Monday, Wednesday and Friday, played in a full court pick-up basketball game on the island's only court, with Officers and enlisted men from the Air Force and Navy, in addition to the Army. One day at our basketball game, during a break we took between halves, I was chatting with an Air Force Lieutenant from the south who I had become friendly with, about a rumor that was going around that two helicopters had crashed and sunk in the Island Lagoon, each costing about $85,000.

"Is that true?" I asked him.

"Sure is," he replied. "An' there's gonna be some more of 'em ditched unless I get transferred out of this hellhole!"

All I know is he didn't show up to play anymore and we never heard of any more helicopters crashing.

The I.Q. scores interested me also because one of my duties under Major Murphy had become reading and making recommendations on applications for Compassionate Leave, made available by an Army Regulation specifying extraordinary home circumstances that could justify usually ten days of leave to straighten out the problem or attend the funeral of a parent, etc. The job was given to me because I was a law graduate, along with instructions that whenever there appeared to be merit to the request, I was to contact by TWIX the local Red Cross or religious leader in the soldier's home town for verification of the alleged crisis. Whatever other problems Murphy had, he was not stupid, and after he rotated, I began to miss him because his replacement was such a disaster. Captain Spalding was very fat, slovenly in his dress, and extremely stupid. Our first encounter occurred when he informed me that he was "also a law graduate" so we had our law training in common. I was suspicious so I politely inquired as to what school he had attended.

"The Augusta, Georgia Night School Law Centre" came the answer. " I have my Certificate but haven't had the time to get it framed yet. You know, Layton, we lawyers have to stick together."

I did not respond. But that night I took a peek at his 201 File and found out how he had become an officer. At the end of WW II, thousands of officers were discharged and returned to civilian life. The Army was short of officers so they gave temporary promotions to numbers of *non-coms*, like Spalding, who had never risen above being a Staff Sergeant during his entire regular Army career. In the event of another real emergency, he would go back to being a Sergeant once again. That is what I was stuck with and to whom I reported in my review of Compassionate Leave applications.

Sure enough after reviewing and checking out dozens of these applications, not one of which I had recommended be approved, since the local Red Cross never found them to be factual, and my common sense told me that some of the letters of the spouse or girl friend were fakes, I finally received an application which really troubled me. It was from a young cook in the Island Mess Hall. He wrote in his application about his wife having fallen for some local carpenter, who was so great in bed that she had to describe

126

all of what it did to her, how many times a night they did "it" and how much she loved it. Accompanying this was a letter from his local pastor to whom he had written and who verified the substance of the story. I typed up a quick TWIX to the local Red Cross in the cook's hometown, along with a memo to Spalding recommending that this Leave Application be granted if the Red Cross backed up the Minister's letter. Back from Spalding came a scrawled note:

"You can't be taken in by these fakers, Layton. Rejected."

This marked the only time I ever argued with an officer over his decision. I tried to explain to Spalding that this was the only application I had ever come across that had a true ring of authenticity to it; I explained that this cook had a military I.Q. score of 78, that I had taken the trouble to interview him and that he was in tears when he spoke to me, and that I feared the worst if we turned him down. His mess hall superiors whom I spoke to agreed with me. I got nowhere. My "legal colleague" was adamant.

"I can always sniff out the phonies!" He said.

So, *we* rejected the application. Two weeks later that young cook swallowed an entire bottle of rat poison in the mess hall. He was taken by emergency helicopter to the

Guam Hospital, but he never made it there alive. I never spoke to Spalding again; all of my communications to him were in writing. He also avoided me wherever possible.

Then one day I received a letter from Janet, who was attending graduate school in New Haven to get an MAT in teaching, suggesting that she would like to contact my mother about making a visit to see her while I was away as they both had my interests in common. I wrote that I thought it a good idea (knowing that my Mother would be thrilled at getting a chance to look her over) and gave her my parent's home phone number. A little while later I received a glowing letter from my Mother telling me all about her visit from Janet, what a lovely girl she was, and that she could not be more pleased (and, of course, she had ascertained that Janet came from a Jewish family living in the Bronx, that her mother was a school teacher for many years and her father a dentist). A similar glowing description of this teacup meeting of my two primary correspondents came from Janet, who told of how much she liked my Mother. I had no idea as to whether one or both of them were lying, but it was clear to me that my days of indecision might well be coming to an end.

Well, I never got a chance to make that decision for some six weeks later I received in the mail what men in the military have often referred to as a "Dear John" letter. It was from Janet, informing me that she could not wait any longer for me to make up my mind about getting married to her and enclosing a clipping from the Sunday *New York Times* announcing her engagement to another Michigan graduate, with a law degree from Columbia, named Irwin Jay Robinson. I was crushed for a long while, no longer getting her letters with new chess moves and gossip about people we knew while dating before I was drafted. I was actually a "short-timer" heading for the November anniversary of my arrival on The Rock and occupied myself with plans for my actual R & R to Japan, saved for as late in my tour as possible.

Stahl had already taken his R & R to Tokyo and filled me in on what to do and not to do, so I hitched up with another of our eight Honolulu travelers, a lawyer from Brooklyn, New York, named Arthur Halpern, who traveled with me and had figured out a way to get an extra five days added to our visit. Our travel orders contained a badly worded phrase that permitted an interpretation that would get us to the airport several hours after the flight to Eniwetok had departed. We were at the end of this awful year and figured that the Army might be too busy to actually go to the trouble of a court-martial, especially with that questionable interpretation being relied on by us. So we decided to gamble.

Everyone of the prior groups who made the Tokyo trip recommended that we take a taxi to a place that called itself the "Officers Club" after landing at the airport and buying some civilian clothes. Without our uniforms on, no one could tell that we weren't officers; and when we got there and registered, we realized that the proprietors of the club didn't care whether we were officers or not, as long as we paid their outrageous room rates. A bevy of fairly pretty Japanese girls were present and joined Arthur and me for drinks and a Japanese dinner. We stayed at the "Club" for most of our R & R, with the interruption of our fake departure to the airport knowingly several hours late, and expressing our disappointment at having missed our flight back to our coral reef home. The Sergeant at the check-in desk hollered at us, said we should be court-martialed, but was troubled by Arthur's strongly argued misinterpretation of the language of the orders. He threw us out and told us he was arranging to get us on a flight to Guam with a connecting short hop to Eniwetok in five days.

"Miss that one and I will make sure you both are court-martialed. Now get out of here," he shouted, and we did; right back to the "Officers Club" for a few more days.

Back on The Rock, I spent the last days of my one-year tour working for the new Island Commander, another West Point Colonel, as his clerk typist. He and I got along quite well until I started bothering him about the fact that I could not find any purchase orders for protective eye glasses to be used by Army personnel when the H-Bomb is tested, while the Air Force, Navy, and Coast Guard had received their glasses weeks ago. He snapped at me that he was tired of hearing from me about this problem.

"You've probably overlooked the order somewhere in the files. I can't believe your predecessor could have made such an error."

Well, it appeared that he did. And when I told my pals in our barracks about this development they were all very upset. The first H-Bomb test was scheduled for three weeks after my plane left for Honolulu and then the States. The men in my barracks wanted my home address in order to write to me if they were blinded by the blast so I could help them sue the Army, or the government. I didn't want to tell them that they couldn't sue their government, or the Army, for injuries suffered in the ordinary course of performing their duties. As Stahl and I had arrived on the same airplane exactly one year ago, we were traveling together on a plane back to the States.

On arrival at a military post at an airport outside San Francisco, we were given orders to return via a civilian flight to New York and to report for further assignment to the Army office on Governor's Island. There we were told of our 30-day leave entitlement, and possible locations for the last days of our two years of active service. As I was a reservist, I had a technical requirement of six more years in the Reserves, which everyone knew was not enforced. Six months more was all I had to serve, but there were no orders yet as to where that would take place. I was told that one of my possible last posts was Fort Slocum, off the coast of New Rochelle in Long Island Sound, but that was not yet decided so I had to wait for a decision. I was released for my 30-day leave and headed for my parents' home, where I was warmly welcomed.

When my leave was over, I reported back to Governor's Island and found out that I had indeed been assigned to Fort Slocum, which I was very happy about since it was driving distance across the Bronx-Whitestone Bridge, up to New Rochelle, and a ferry ride across to the Fort each morning, and I could sleep at my parent's home each night.

I was assigned to the only active unit there, a T & E outfit, which appeared to have nothing to do. I worked for a

Sergeant, who mostly watched television during the day, then left early in the afternoon, leaving me to answer the phone, fill out crossword puzzles, and read books. While doing that, I studiously researched what was termed "Early Discharge" available under the still extant G.I. Bill for returning servicemen who claimed the need to complete their interrupted education.

What I needed was a course that started during the summer and that would only last some three weeks, thus getting me out of the Army some three months early. DeRusso would have been proud of me, for the scheme worked. I found, almost unbelievably, a perfect course offering at the NYU Business School, summer session, second half, that dealt with successful business plans and the reason they worked. The dates for the course offering worked perfectly, I completed all the Army application forms, easily got my Sergeant to approve the request and then just waited for my early discharge in order to "complete my education." All went well and I was discharged three months early during the summer. The course was actually interesting as we studied the business methods of the then hugely successful "Chock Full of Nuts" coffee chain in Manhattan. I also picked up all of the required forms for completing my application for admission to the New York bar from the Appellate Division, Second Department in Brooklyn, and started on the tedious task of getting affidavits from every employer I had since the age of 17.

So, from the rain and misery of Fort Dix in the fall of 1954 until the summer of 1956, I completed my dreaded military service, without getting court-martialed once, and receiving a spotless Discharge, returned to civilian life.

13

Searching for My First Law Job

After having been sworn in as a member of the New York Bar in October of 1956, I began a job search in the midst of a mild recession. I started by contacting my law school's Placement Office, which described a job opening it had received from one of the school's alumni named Richard Goldwater, at a small NYC firm named Goldwater & Flynn, located at 60 E. 42nd Street in the Lincoln Building.

I applied and was hired at the munificent salary of $75 per week, apparently then the going rate for non-Wall Street firms. Fortuitously, I found that one of my female classmates, Anne Gross, had been there since graduation, not having to worry about being drafted. She greeted me and said she would be glad to show me the ropes, even though neither I, nor any of my male classmates, had ever opened a door for her during three years at Yale Law School. When I said I was unaware that I had been rude, she chuckled and said she would help me anyway.

I rapidly discovered that there was not much real legal work to be done there. There were only three associates: Anne, myself, and a young fellow from Boston named Ed

Bloom. We each were often sent to State Supreme Court to answer calendar calls and ask for a brief adjournment, mostly to spare the partners from having to do so. I was once sent to Albany on a Friday afternoon as time was running out to file very important documents for a new housing project for clients of Monroe Goldwater, a Senior Partner, which I was able to file before the offices closed. The other partners were Ed Flynn, the other Senior Partner, and James and Richard Goldwater, the sons of Monroe.

When there were no trips to the Courthouse or Albany, we sat in the library, since there were no individual offices for us, and tried to teach ourselves the intricacies of the Civil Practice Law & Rules (CPLR) in order to avoid total boredom—or we chatted with each other, mostly listening to tales by Ed of his drinking experiences and the characters he met each evening at his favorite Madison Avenue bar.

As this routine soon became quite boring, was getting me nowhere since I was learning very little, and had been there almost a year, I thought it time to renew contact with Professor McDougal, for whom I had been a Research Assistant at Yale Law School. He had encouraged me to keep in touch with him, as he had done with other of what were loosely termed "Mac's Boys", who he liked to place in positions of import around the world and keep in touch with just in case he needed a favor.

I had corresponded with him from Eniwetok when he was writing a major law review article on the subject of the Hydrogen Bomb Tests that were to take place there. I phoned him and explained my situation briefly and he asked that I come up to New Haven. I did so on a Saturday morning and found him, as usual, quite hearty, friendly and decisive.

"I told you when you were working for me that you should consider going into law teaching," he said.

"But I wasn't on the Law Review and have never taught before," I replied.

"Nonsense. You are plenty smart enough to teach law."

"But who would hire me?" I asked.

"That's my job," he said. "You just think it over and decide if you want to give it a try. On your way out, just leave your address and phone number with my secretary, and I'll do the rest."

I thanked him and said I would be thinking it over, and returned to New York.

Several days later I received a telegram from a professor at the Stanford Law School in Palo Alto, California offering me a position as a Teaching Fellow at Stanford for the 1957-1958 academic year at a salary of

$7,500, almost twice what I was making at Goldwater & Flynn. I thought it over and realized it was an opportunity I could not turn down, whether I decided to continue a teaching career or not. I had to break out of my dead-end situation. I was sad to bid goodbye to Anne and Ed, then phoned Mac to thank him, accepted the offer by telephone so I could find out when to arrive in time to find an apartment before classes began. I then headed west in my new Chevy Bel Air convertible. My good friend, Norm Brock, from college days at Michigan, accompanied me from Detroit to San Francisco. We had a great trip viewing the wonders of the Grand Canyon and other famous sites.

At Stanford, I worked for Professor Harold Shepherd, well known for his casebook and writings on Contracts, and also taught a required freshman course on Legal Writing, as did the two other Teaching Fellows hired with me that year. I also became friendly, while at the Stanford gym playing pick-up basketball games, with Lester Mazor, a third-year student who was one of the editors of the *Stanford Law Review*, who I saw in later life in Washington, D.C. and during summers in Lenox, Massachusetts.

As the academic year was drawing to a close and since I had decided not to accept the offer of a professorship at Stanford as it was tied into a five-year contract, and I did wish to return to the eastern seaboard, I signed up to attend the Annual Meeting of the Association of American Law Schools, taking place in Chicago. It was informally known as the "Meat Market" for it was the place where law professors looked for new jobs. You might be interviewed while sitting next to a potted plant in the hotel lobby or in a Dean's hotel room. I did have a very encouraging interview with the Dean of the Buffalo Law School, who invited me to visit there at the school's expense after the Meat Market.

While in Buffalo, I received a call from Professor Phil Neal at Stanford, who had been on sabbatical leave that year. Despite having never met me, he told me he had heard good reports from others on the faculty about me. He was calling because a close friend of his, Malcolm Wilkey, who had graduated with him from Harvard Law School, had just been appointed Assistant Attorney General in charge of the Office of Legal Counsel at the Department of Justice and wanted to hire two very bright young lawyers with a year or so of experience in order to put his stamp on the office. He gave me the number to call to arrange for an interview appointment by stopping off on my return to Palo Alto. It would not cost much more since I could simply change my reservation to take a flight to Washington, stay for the interview, catch a later flight to San Francisco, then return to Palo Alto. I didn't see how it could hurt to take the interview, especially as Buffalo was cruelly cold in the winter. Buffalo did offer me an Assistant Professorship, Still, my gut told me to go to Washington for the interview.

I was very favorably impressed with Malcolm Wilkey and Paul Sweeney, his First Assistant. The job and the location were also attractive. So, I accepted the offer made to me by Mr. Wilkey, and would soon be heading to D.C. for the next three years.

14

The Department of Justice Under Eisenhower and Kennedy

Arriving at the Office of Legal Counsel in May of 1958, I was greeted warmly and assigned to share an office—on a temporary basis—with a young Harvard Law graduate who had recently completed his military service in the Marine Corps. His name was Donald Green and we got along quite well, becoming good friends over the next few years.

Much of the initial work assigned to both of us was library based legal research. For example, one of the duties of the head of the Office had been, and continued to be, the preparation and issuance of Opinions of the Attorney General, when there were disputes between government agencies or Departments as to the meaning or interpretation of a statute, or the powers of one Agency when challenged by the claimed jurisdiction of another Department or Agency.

Much of this was dull on the surface, but when one flashes forward to future administrations, the work we had to do showed a careful and honest Administration, respectful of the law. By contrast, almost half a century later, under the leadership of George W. Bush, it was discovered that this very Office had been manned by carefully selected ideologues willing to compromise long-held legal principles in order to issue Opinions sanctioning the Administration's use of "waterboarding" and other violent methods of witness interrogation in violation of long-standing international agreements to which the United States was a signatory. The entire legal academy expressed dismay and indignation in Letters to the Editor of major newspapers signed by hundreds of law professors from leading law schools. One or two of the offending Opinion writers did resign amid the outcry, admitting that the pressures placed upon them to comply with the Administration's wishes had been difficult to resist.

As time went on and the head of our Office, Malcolm R. Wilkey, and his principal Assistant, Paul Sweeney, grew more confident in our legal abilities, we were given more demanding and independent assignments. Some of it was speechwriting on a statute or treaty on which we had expertise. Occasionally, it was to comment on or to draft amendments to legislation pending before the Congress and in which the Department of Justice had a direct interest. Frequently, it was to review either proposed lawsuits recommended by the Civil Rights Division, or legislation proposed by that Division, largely because the issue of civil rights was looming large on the front pages of most American newspapers and might well be an issue in the upcoming Presidential election. Until the first half of 1960, I had never had any direct contact with the Attorney General, William P. Rogers, but that changed when one morning, Don and I, who now had offices of our own, were summoned to meet with him in his enormous office, which was not far down the 5th floor corridor from most of the Legal Counsel offices.

We introduced ourselves and Mr. Rogers was gracious in stating that he had occasion to read much of our written output and that it was because of the excellence of the research and writing that he was now giving us a confidential assignment. President Eisenhower, he explained, was reaching the end of his second term in office, and questions had arisen in his mind about certain provisions of the U.S. Constitution. The President had put these queries to him in his capacity as his legal adviser, choosing to circumvent the White House Counsel for reasons of his own. Mr. Rogers stated that he was going to assign two of these questions to each of us and wanted a thorough legal analysis prepared for transmittal directly to him and on a strictly confidential basis, with a review by Mr. Wilkey, and thereafter transmittal to the President.

The questions assigned to me were:

1. Why do appointments by the President to certain positions, such as the head of the U.S. Atomic Energy Commission, require the "advice and consent of the Senate" (Article 2, Section 2)?

2. What is the purpose of and the need for the Electoral College (Article 2, Section 1)?

The questions assigned to Don Green related to the several methods for amending the Constitution specified in *Article V.* Eisenhower was probably interested in this because he wanted to see some new amendments adopted, or old ones changed.

We returned to our respective offices and thence to the Department Library to commence days of research and writing. One of my pieces, I recall, was at least 70 pages long, and the other not much shorter. The Advice and Consent issue clearly was raised due to Eisenhower's frustration at not having been able to secure the Senate's consent to his appointment of Admiral Lewis Strauss to head the Atomic Energy Commission due to the opposition of many Democrats caused by his fund-raising prowess on behalf of the Republican party. The existence of the Electoral College appeared to any intelligent reader an entirely unnecessary appendage that could only be designed to upset the result of an election by some form of trickery. So it was easy to understand the President's thoughtfulness in asking these questions.

My work was reviewed by Malcolm Wilkey who made few changes, complimented me on the products and passed the memoranda on to the Attorney General, as I assume was done with Don's pieces. Nothing was heard on this subject for some weeks, when, once again, we were both called to the AG's office, told by him not to be upset, but were required to now redo our work on one page for each subject, as the President—we were now informed—never cared to read anything longer than one page in length! We were dumbfounded; having become so enthralled with the intricacies of our endeavor, but nonetheless, resigned ourselves to the rewriting.

In truth, I found the abbreviated version not only a challenge, but also a learning process. I realized that much of what I had written was historical, analytical, and filled with unnecessary anecdote.

During this entire period I was always aware that the memoranda I wrote retained my name as author and that when controversy arose over a subject with one of the independent agencies or other offices and a meeting took place to resolve it, I was usually invited to attend by

Mr. Wilkey or Mr. Sweeney. On one such occasion, the Memorandum I had written on the desire of the Commonwealth of Puerto Rico to apply for statehood had been sent to Abe Fortas, the Commonwealth's counsel (and future Supreme Court Justice during the Kennedy Administration), who violently objected to it. A meeting was scheduled and I was, as standard practice, invited to attend. Mr. Fortas was extremely angered by the conclusions reached in my Memorandum, which had become the principal topic of discussion, and he ended the meeting by hurling his copy of the Memorandum onto the table, saying "We'll see who wins this one after I talk to the White House!" and stalked out of the room. Parenthetically, he did prevail, as the White House counsel informed us a week later.

In contrast, when the Kennedy Administration took over the Justice Department, our names never remained on our work product and we were never invited to attend meetings to discuss the controversies we had analyzed in writing. Rarely, if ever, did we learn of the outcome of an issue.

Some weeks after having turned in our one-page revisions, I listened to, and then read quite carefully, President Eisenhower's Farewell Address to the nation, which contained his memorable warning about the potential dangers of what he termed the activities of "the military-industrial complex". Little heed was initially paid to this former General's warnings, but in recent years many pundits have complimented Eisenhower's prescience regarding the subject. In a curious footnote to history, a box of misplaced notes by a speechwriter, Malcolm Moos, was found lying in a boathouse in Hackensack, Minnesota, which contained the original notations on the speech, reflecting the many revisions to that language insisted upon by Eisenhower despite objections from Moos. **(See December 2010 issue, *The New Yorker*, "The Talk of the Town, Ike's Speech").**

The incident regarding his late-term interest in provisions of the Constitution also served to remind me of his request some years earlier for a Report on what the Federal government could do to prevent the recurrence of an embarrassing scandal on a nationally watched TV program called "The 64 Thousand Dollar Question." A college professor named Charles Van Doren, son of nationally known Columbia University professor Mark Van Doren, had been caught cheating by receiving the answers to difficult questions from the program's producers. I had been assigned the writing of such a report due to

Eisenhower's desire to assure the public that such an occurrence would never be repeated. All of us knew that no Federal statute protected against this kind of conduct, but I was told to "come up with something" and did so, with the help of a former colleague at OLC, who was then on the staff of the Federal Communications Commission. We proposed several different approaches to changes in the F.C.C. statute, while knowing full well that the TV industry would never permit the passage of any of the legislation that we proposed. It was a cosmetic job, nicely bound, thousands of copies were run off, it was widely circulated, and I was informed that the President was satisfied.

It was not long after the incident involving Ike's queries about the Constitution that John Kennedy won the 1960 election and my encounters with the new Attorney General took a sharply different turn.

15

The Spirit of Valley Forge and Monte Casino

From my hiring in May of 1958 through the 1960 Presidential Election won by John F. Kennedy, I had prospered as a young Attorney-Adviser on the staff of the Office of Legal Counsel (OLC) at the Department of Justice. The new president's appointment of his younger brother, Robert F. Kennedy, to be his Attorney General was a shocking piece of news, greeted with incredulity by virtually all of the members of the OLC staff.

Our recent Attorneys General had been Herbert Brownell, a distinguished New York City lawyer, senior partner in a major Wall Street firm, who inaugurated the Honors Program at the Department of Justice, which was the vehicle by which I and many others had been recruited into government service, followed by William P. Rogers, another prominent member of the New York bar, who had come to Justice from the firm of Rogers & Wells, which he headed. I was particularly distressed by the appointment as I had followed the scurrilous machinations of the late Senator Joseph R. McCarthy during my final year at law school and knew that Robert Kennedy had been his Chief Counsel who assisted in conducting a campaign of reckless vilification against many innocent employees of the Federal government. How he could be qualified to head the U.S. Department of Justice was a mystery and a cruel joke to me. I realized that my tenure at the Department might be short-lived unless my observations of young Mr. Kennedy had been off the mark. Events soon proved my fears to have been accurate.

My first encounter with our new Attorney General took place in mid-January of 1961 when it was announced that he had scheduled a meeting with all the members of the OLC legal staff, 12 attorneys, on a sunny Wednesday morning. Twelve chairs had been arranged in a semicircle in front of the huge desk in the overly spacious office used by all U.S. Attorneys General, and he started the meeting by telling us how impressed he was by what he had learned about the history and traditions of our office. He then said that he wanted to get to know us by having each of us speak in turn, starting from his right, stating name, length of time in the Office, specialized areas of expertise, if any, name of law school, year of graduation, and class rank on graduation. This, from someone most of us knew from press accounts, had graduated in the bottom of his class at the University of Virginia Law School.

There followed some embarrassing moments when

older members of the office had to recite their fairly modest law school backgrounds, as they were largely products of the 1930's depression era. I was next to the last to speak, sitting next to a young lady who was our most recent hire of several weeks ago. I informed him that I was hired in May of 1958, specialized in public international law as well as civil rights issues, and had graduated in 1954 from the Yale Law School in the top quarter of my class. The young lady sitting next to me recited her short tenure since being hired only two weeks ago upon graduation from Georgetown Law School, where she had ranked first in her class. There was a smattering of chuckles when Kennedy then said, with apparent pride in his sense of humor, that "Perhaps, Mary, it would be best if you and I exchanged seats." Unquestionably, many of us thought that was a fine idea, but kept dutifully quiet.

My next encounter, not with our hero, but involving him, took place several weeks later, on the occasion of the Washington's Birthday holiday—a traditional closing of government offices—and bargain shopping at Woodward & Lothrop and Garfinkel's, which department stores both had Washington's Birthday sales. I took that occasion to drive my Chevy Bel Air convertible into the Justice Department garage that morning as it was the only time that one could do so since during regular work days all spaces were reserved for high-ranking officials and FBI big shots. The garage was mostly empty that holiday when I entered, then went up to my office, completed my Federal and D.C. income tax returns in a couple of hours, walked over to the department store sales where I bought some bargains, returned to the garage for my car, and buzzed on home.

The following morning, a regular workday, I found a phone message from the secretary of my immediate superior, the third ranking official in OLC, requesting my presence in his office at once. On entering, I was confronted by his asking:

"What were you doing here yesterday, Layton?"

"My Federal and D.C. taxes, Harold. Then, I walked over to the sales in town."

"I thought so," he replied.

"And now I have to give you a letter of commendation from our brilliant new AG for diligence beyond the call of ordinary duty in working on a Federal holiday. Obviously, his public relations office will be issuing a press release about all of you hard workers who toiled here on Washington's Birthday."

"But Harold, how did they know I was here?"

"He had the FBI take down all the license plate

numbers from the cars in the garage and look up the owners; and so here is your Letter of Commendation. Do with it what you will. Now get out of here!"

I suppressed my laughter and left quickly as I knew Harold Reis had little regard for the public relations exploits of politicians.

Several of my contemporaries had used the garage for similar purposes and received similar letters. They decided to embarrass Kennedy by leaking the story to *The Washington Post*, which published a two-paragraph box about the incident on its front page. The top brass were furious and immediately caused all offices to have the letters returned in order that they could be destroyed and a new inquiry was made so that those who actually worked on the holiday, of which there were many, could receive replacement letters. I complied and returned my letter.

Amusingly, 32 years later, historian Richard Reeves published his version of John Kennedy's shortened presidency, entitled "President Kennedy: Profile of Power," which I was interested to read, having served in his administration for some four months. I was mystified to find on page 66 of that volume, a description of the above noted incident that was totally distorted and which blamed FBI Director J. Edgar Hoover for having sent a note to

Robert Kennedy thanking him for coming to work on February 22nd, a national holiday, after having observed his car in the Department garage. The note allegedly went on to state:

> "The spirit you demonstrated—the spirit of Valley Forge and Monte Casino—will, we hope, spread through the entire Department of Justice. Keep up the good work."

Robert Kennedy, according to Reeves, was using the note to show his brother that Hoover was a psycho and shouldn't be reappointed as head of the FBI. I realized that something had gone very wrong in Reeves' research and I wrote him a short letter care of his publisher, Simon & Schuster. Amazingly, several weeks later I received a telephone call from Reeves in California at my law office in New York, asking me if I still had my letter of commendation from Kennedy. I told him that it had been taken back and destroyed, but I offered to get him a copy of one that was reissued to one of my classmates, Howard Glickstein, who I knew had worked all of February 22nd, and who had received the re-issued version after having satisfied the "letter police" that he deserved it. Reeves asked me to try to get a copy of that letter from my classmate, who I found, not only had kept it, but had it framed on his office wall. I asked Howard to make a copy of the letter and to mail it directly to Reeves, whose address at Stanford University I gave to him. Reeves was extremely grateful and later wrote me to explain that the error was caused by his research assistant, who had lifted a passage from Arthur Schlesinger's *Robert Kennedy and His Times*, wherein Schlesinger incorrectly described the note as having been sent by Edgar Hoover to Robert Kennedy. The origin of the reference to "Valley Forge and Monte Casino" is unknown except, one assumes, to Arthur Schlesinger. Jr.

Richard Reeves corrected the story in a later edition of his book and credited me and my classmate in a footnote. To me, one of the lessons learned from the incident, apart from the character of Robert F. Kennedy, is the fact that historians sometimes do not do their own original research, relying rather on research assistants, who also do not do their own research, but copy passages from prior publications, without having verified their accuracy at all. The incidents above described were not, however, the final disappointing encounters I had with our new Attorney General prior to leaving government service.

Flushing, NY 1945

Don Holden and me in front of Flushing High School where we
jointly wrote a humor column for the school newspaper.
Don went on to attend Columbia College
while I went to the University of Michigan.

Eniwetok - 1955

Facing away from an atomic blast.

Headquarters Company JTF7 on Eniwetok.
A very long year!

The Hague - 1960

Krzysz Skubiszewski, George Abi-Saab,
George Ofosu-Amaah and Hisashi Owada

Hans Blix, Elihu Lauterpacht and Krzysz Skubiszewski

George Ofosu-Amaah, Krzysz Skubiszewski,
me and Hisashi Owada

Geneva, Switzerland: 1978

Edward Pauk, Jake Parker and me

Eliot Humrich, Cal Elliott, Maurice Brooks and me

Fred Sherman and Maurice Brooks

The Geneva Water Spout (140 meters high)

Me and Krzysz Skubiszewski, 1963
in front of the UN Headquarters, New York City

Malcolm R. Wilkey,
Assistant Attorney General in charge of the Office of Legal Counsel,
1958-1960

Professor Myers McDougal, Yale Law School

16

Diploma of The Hague Academy of International Law

In the spring of 1959, I received a Memo from the head of the Office of Legal Counsel at Justice, Mr. Wilkey, inquiring whether I would be interested in attending that summer's session of the Hague Academy of International Law, since public as well as private international law were subjects that I had specialized in, both in law school and during the course of my work. The attached material furnished by The Hague Academy made clear that attendees could simply attend the Main Lecture Series (to be given that year by Professor Quincy Wright of the University of Virginia Law School) or sit for the written and oral examinations in order to qualify for the Diploma of the Academy.

The Memo from Mr. Wilkey specified that Administrative Leave was available (as well as transportation and room and board paid for by the Carnegie Endowment for International Peace) to a lawyer sent from our Office, but only if he or she agreed to sit for the Diploma. I thought it over with care, researched the activities and reputation of the Academy, and decided that, since taking exams was something I had been doing for most of my life, two more would not hurt me. Moreover, a summer in The Hague was a hard vacation to turn down. Before I knew it, I was on my way to the continent again, some nine years after my youthful experience at Oxford.

Upon arrival at The Hague, when I checked in at the desk at the Academy building, I was informed that I was being put up with other students at a dormitory maintained by the Peace Palace, directly across the road. It was suggested that I take the daily, guided tour of the Peace Palace to view the courtroom used by the Justices of the International Court of Justice (ICJ), an organ of the United Nations. I was familiar with the ICJ since the United States Senate was still engaged in heated debate over U.S. accession to its jurisdiction. I took the tour, and was immensely impressed by all of the trappings of the Peace Palace, and even the Lecture Room of the Academy and its Library.

I had read parts of Quincy Wright's treatise on public international law while doing research in the Department library, but hearing him in person each day for the three weeks of the General Course was a great pleasure for me. I had no doubt that some of his subject matter would be on the examination as he was one of the three academics who supervised and graded the Diploma examinations. During one or two of the cocktail events arranged by the Academy, I was able to chat briefly with him and realized how friendly and affable a person he was.

At the student dormitory, I made friends with a collection of interesting attendees. One, Jim Brachman, a Harvard Law School graduate, and the only other American sitting for the Diploma, told me that he was determined to win one as it would assist him in getting a better job in the States. Brachman also believed that the record of Americans in passing the written exam was not very good, and that only those who passed it were even permitted to qualify for the oral exam. There was a Chinese student who studied for endless hours in the Library, as well as participants from several other European countries. I also made friends with a Belgian girl, somewhat pretty, whose serious limp didn't at all impede her ability to drive her Peugeot, in which she was willing to drive me around. She was a lawyer, not sitting for the exams but interested in meeting bright men; she knew a lot about the exams from having attended the General Course during the previous summer, and gave me some invaluable advice.

She said that most American law students or lawyers were used to "issue spotting" exam questions; and did not understand that European academics were looking for historical analyses in a written examination. She said, first you must write a general historical description of the area of inquiry, and then pose the question to be answered. Then you must write a short history of the subject matter, with as many references to historical events as possible. Only then must you attempt to suggest solutions to the question posed, and lastly you must refer the reader back to the original inquiry as though you were closing this academic circle. I thanked her very much and did not disclose any of her suggestions.

When the General Course ended, many of the dormitory tenants departed, leaving only the grinds preparing for the exams. There were about twenty of us to my recollection, ignoring each other while getting more nervous each day. Finally, the written exam was given, and I realized from the three questions posed that my lady friend's advice was right on the mark. So, I wrote as she directed, using as much of my historical recollection of Wright's lecture materials as possible. The following morning, posted on the board at the Academy entrance hall were the names of the eight candidates for the Diploma who had passed the written examination. Mine was there listed alphabetically.

The oral examination took place the next afternoon

before three well-known professors of public international law, chaired by Professor Wright. There was also an audience of local lawyers and law students, as well as those taking the oral exam. By that time, I had much experience speaking on my feet, from my neophyte immersion at the Barrister's Union mock trial, to arguing a Department of Justice tax appeal in the Second Circuit Court of Appeals in New York, to arguing orally with opposing lawyers from different government agencies, I enjoyed public speaking. Thus, I had no problems with any of the questions put to me by the panel of judges during the oral exam. On the other hand, the Chinese candidate, who had studied like a madman could only stammer his way through to public failure. Three of the eight oral finalists were awarded the Diploma. I was told that I was only the fourth American ever to have been awarded one.

Several of my friends who still were in The Hague took me out to a farewell lunch at a local well-regarded bistro and insisted that I order a local specialty called "steak tartar", which was then unknown to me. When it arrived, I realized that it was uncooked and I just couldn't bring myself to eat it. With my permission, they devoured my order with relish.

From The Hague, I journeyed to Amsterdam and took a

flight to Geneva. I had telephoned a friend and classmate from Yale, Alan Gladstone who worked for the International Labor Organization in Geneva and had married his childhood girlfriend from Brooklyn, who had just joined him there. They kindly invited me to spend a couple of days with them before I made my last stop in Zurich to visit an old friend from Stanford at his family's lakeside home and renew our rivaling tennis friendship.

When I returned to work in Washington, Malcolm Wilkey seemed pleased that I had won the Diploma. I think he thought of it as an accomplishment for the Office. Apart from that, and my invitation to The Hague the following year to attend a Research Centre, the benefit of the Diploma has never seemed to have been more than another line on my résumé. Perhaps I am wrong and the Diploma has helped me in ways unknown.

During the winter and spring, I wrote an article for the *Stanford Law Review* at the request of its Articles and Book Review Editor, Lester Mazor, the former student of mine, as I had worked on its subject matter as part of my office duties. Entitled *The Dilemma of the World Court: The United States Reconsiders Compulsory Jurisdiction*, the article detailed the strategy surrounding the downfall of the Bricker Amendment, and was well received.

17

"Six O'clock, Monday in My Office"

Following the Washington's Birthday commendation letter fiasco, none of us heard from the new Attorney General for a while. But then came a short memo to each of the current members of the Department's Honors Program who were eligible for departure from May onward due to their completion of three years of service. It invited the recipient to attend a meeting at 6 o'clock Monday in his office in order to discuss the possible terms for extending our three-year service period; and specified that we should enter his office through a door marked "Private-AG Only" on the fifth floor.

Several of us who were friends, discussed the memo prior to the meeting and admitted to each other that if some terms were changed, mostly relating to salary, or reimbursement for out of pocket expenses, we would consider extending our service period, since by and large, we enjoyed the work we were doing and thought its performance had a certain importance. The best example of that was one in our group named Gordon Spivack, also a Yale Law School graduate, who had spent his three years in the Antitrust Division working on one complaint, which was close to being filed. He told us he would welcome being around during the life of that case, or part of it.

As we entered the designated room that Monday evening, we were greeted by the Attorney General, shirt collar unbuttoned, tie askew, not wearing his suit jacket, and holding a bottle of liquor in each hand.

"What'll you have? Scotch, bourbon, gin, or beer?"

I could have predicted one of the responses, which was:

"Mr. Kennedy, Federal regulations prohibit the usage of alcoholic beverages on Federal property," which drew the response, "I'll have to speak to my brother about changing that. Don't worry about it—Now, what'll you have…scotch, bourbon?"

None of us was willing to drink anything other than a soft drink, mostly Cokes.

When the meeting started, Kennedy explained his purpose in asking us to consider extending our terms of service.

"You're all doing important work, important for our country. My goal is to get you to stay on and continue going after the rascals who are hell-bent on ruining it. These monsters have to be put out of business."

Mostly, we were confused, and weren't sure who he was talking about.

One voice was heard saying, "Who are you talking about, Mr. Kennedy?"

"Why, Hoffa, of course", came the reply. "He and his mobster pals have got to be indicted, convicted and kept in jail!"

One of us then countered: "But only one or two of us are in the Criminal Division; the rest are in Civil, Civil Appellate, Civil Rights, Deputy AG, Legal Counsel, Admiralty, Solicitor General, etc. and have nothing to do with Hoffa and company."

"OK, OK, that's correct, but that's just my best example. The important thing is for you all not to leave now."

Spivack spoke up, "We understand what you are saying and many of us would like to stay on, but our pay has to be dealt with. Our contemporaries who are working for large law firms are making perhaps $10,000 more a year, plus they get dinner money when they work late, garage charges reimbursed, even babysitter expenses paid for. It all adds up and we don't get any of that. We're not asking for all of that, but something better than the pay grade we've been stuck at for the last three years."

"Well, let me think it over," said Kennedy, and "We'll meet again next Monday; same time; same place."

There were about twelve of us at this first meeting, and we all agreed to be back the next week to see what the President's brother would come up with. The next Monday arrived and he started off again with the same liquor offerings, which we turned down.

Then he said, "I've given our discussion of last week a lot of thought and think I have something you'll like. We're going to start a Department of Justice Law Review. You'll each be able to publish an article on your subject of choice that will be read by everyone in the Department and probably others—all paid for by the Department."

We were all amazed. Spivack could not control himself, and in his usual outspoken style, said, "A law review? You must be kidding! Do more research and writing for no more pay? Most of us wrote for our Reviews in law school. You must think we're idiots. No more of these meetings for me. I've had a standing offer from the Cahill Gordon firm in New York for whenever I'm ready to leave but I didn't want to take it because I've been working here on a good case against A & P Supermarkets. That's the conglomerate that put my parents' little neighborhood grocery store out of business. But it's not fair to my wife and kids to hold out any longer. So long guys."

And with that he left.

Kennedy didn't blink. "So, who's ready to sign up for the Department Law Review?"

No hands went up. "Well, I'll have to take another look and talk to you guys next Monday."

The next Monday was our last Monday. When we

arrived, the liquor offer was rebuffed as usual. But this time he outdid himself. His new-and last-proposal was "Department of Justice Continuing Education Classes" in the evenings. As pointed out by some of my few colleagues left in attendance, this would be on top of, and in addition to our regular assignments, again, for no extra pay and probably even cause some to have to spring for taxi fare to get home late in the evening.

"He's nuts" was one of the kinder comments made by my fellow Honors Program colleagues as we each left the room—and then the Department—within weeks thereafter.

I interviewed for several government Agency jobs that had not yet been filled by Kennedy campaign workers or major financial contributors with inside influence. The only one that I was offered was as the Personal Assistant to the soon-to-be-outgoing General Counsel of the Department of Defense, and even I could figure out that as soon as the Kennedys got around to appointing a new General Counsel, he would pick his own Personal Assistant, and the effort was not worth it for another line on a résumé, and having to start the search all over again.

A startup law firm of three Yale Law School grads from a class five years earlier than mine interviewed me with enthusiasm and made me an offer to become their first associate. Stupidly, I turned it down when I was recommended to the departing Republican Assistant

Attorney General in charge of the Civil Rights Division—
one Harold R. Tyler, who interviewed me and offered me a
job back in New York at his former firm, Gilbert & Segall,
where he had been and again would be in charge of all their
litigation. He made an unconditional promise to teach me
how to try civil jury cases—and I believed him. Plus, I
must confess, that after a year at Stanford Law School and
three at the Department in D.C., I kind of looked forward to
seeing my parents again, who were getting on in years, and
to living back in the Big Apple.

So, I packed most of my stuff into my Chevy Bel Air
convertible, shipping the rest via Railway Express, and
drove home following an extended absence to start what I
was looking forward to as my career as a trial lawyer.

18

Almost Becoming a Spook

As the summer approached, I received a letter from the Carnegie Institute stating that, as a new holder of the Diploma, I was invited to become a member of the Research Centre to be held at The Hague Academy during the Fall of 1960 under the direction of Professor Elihu Lauterpacht of Cambridge University. Once again, the Institute covered transportation and expenses. The only requirement was that I produce a publishable article, under the guidance of Professor Lauterpacht, on a subject of public international law. After a brief discussion with Mr. Wilkey as to another Administrative Leave, once again, I left for The Hague, this time to arrive in mid-September for a ten-week stay.

On learning that there were funds available for each attendee to rent a small apartment from among a list maintained by the Academy, I chose one about a ten-minute drive from the Academy. My thought was to rent a bicycle and join the thousands of Dutch men and women who cycled to work each day. But I opted out and took the tram or walked through parks and streets to the Peace Palace and the Academy.

At the first meeting, I learned that several members of the Centre were candidates for an advanced degree in Public International Law at Cambridge and were both students and friends of Professor Lauterpacht.

Like me, others were employees of their national government, involved in the area of public international law. There were employees of the Japanese Foreign Office, the Czech Foreign Ministry, the Swedish Foreign Service, Romanian, Polish, etc., together with the Cambridge students, for a total of twelve of us. It was an exceptionally talented group, all completely fluent in English.

Our meetings began at 10 a.m. and ended at 1 p.m. for the day. Lunch and the Academy library were the agenda for most of us thereafter. When I inquired as to whether there were any local tennis courts, one of my colleagues, a fellow named Zdenek Cervenka, from Czechoslovakia, overheard my inquiries and asked if I needed a partner.

I replied that I certainly did. He said that he knew that there was a small Tennis Club with excellent courts in the nearby seaside village of Scheveningen, but we would need a car to get there and back.

Cervenka appeared to care a great deal about creature comforts that were available in the West and not in his country. He was also determined at some point to bring his wife and child with him out of Czechoslovakia, which he was eventually successful at accomplishing.

He was also more entrepreneurial than I and suggested that we join forces in buying a cheap Austin sedan, which we could use, among other things, as transport to the Club and back, and which we could then sell at the end of the Research Centre for a profit we would split. I asked how much money we would need and he replied that he was sure he could find a car for no more than $300 US dollars. I replied that such a sum was within my budget and he asked that I put that sum into our partnership up front, for which I would receive a higher split on the sale of the car, and I agreed. The next afternoon he took me to look at a black Austin, 4-speed shift car of an older vintage but which seemed to run fine, which he had already bargained down to a price of $250 US dollars. So, on sunny days we usually disappeared from the Library and headed for a couple of hours of fun at our Club. In this manner, Zdenek and I became rather close friends. When the Centre ended, we sold the Austin for $500 and I told Zdenek we would split the profits 50/50.

Elihu Lauterpacht was the only son of Sir Hersch Lauterpacht, a world-renowned authority on public international law and the author of the major treatise on the subject. Eli, as his students and friends knew him, was following in his father's direct footsteps.

A Fellow of Trinity College at Cambridge, he was becoming a recognized specialist in large boundary dispute arbitrations, as well as a lead counsel for large oil companies in their international boundary, and commercial arbitration disputes. He was also married to a very beautiful ballet dancer with whom he had two lively children.

The entire class was invited for cocktails at his local residence and met his wife, who was incredibly shy and quiet, even appearing somewhat troubled. A week or so later the High Jewish Holiday of Yom Kippur took place. While I was as far from a practicing Jew as one could get, I thought it would be nice to attend the New Year service in Holland, and inquired as to the location of a nearby temple. Following the instructions I received, I located the temple. While waiting in line to gain entrance, I found myself standing in front of Eli and his parents. He introduced me, saying he would have invited me to join his family in their seating section had he known that I was a Jew but he had been misled by my name. In the following weeks, our meeting at the synagogue became a bond between us.

The discussions in our seminar were at an extraordinarily high level, challenging our minds, and making the choice of a research topic quite difficult. I finally settled on the subject of "Measures Short of War" in the Law of Treaties, where it appeared that little writing had taken place. Eli approved the choice, but expressed some doubts as to whether sufficient authorities existed to warrant a publishable article. I went to the Library for hours each afternoon (when the weather precluded tennis) and I spent my evenings there as well as I had no social life.

By the time the Research Centre concluded, I had a first draft of my article approved by Eli, on the understanding that I would make all of his suggested changes before submitting it for consideration by any academic publisher, and would consult with him prior to any major changes in direction.

In addition to other members of the Centre, I became friendly with George Ofosu-Amaah from Ghana, who expected to be sent to New York to work at the United Nations on behalf of his government—with Krzysz Skubiszewski from the Polish Foreign Affairs Ministry, and Hans Blix of the Swedish Ministry of Foreign Affairs. Hans, in later years, became world renowned as head of the UN group that disputed the Bush Administration's claims that Iraq had weapons of mass destruction. Our Japanese colleague, Hisashi Owada, became Japanese Ambassador to the United States at one point in his career, but more famously, was the father of the bride of the new Japanese Emperor, for which she, rather unhappily, had to give up a promising career as an outstanding international economist.

We all agreed on parting, to exchange addresses and phone numbers, and to try to stay in touch with each other, which only occasionally happened.

Many of my Centre colleagues from small countries reached very high positions in their governments. Still, I did have the ability in our society of earning much more money than they. I also noticed that no women were represented at the Centre.

On my return to Washington and work at the Office of Legal Counsel, I witnessed the Presidential election of 1960, which John Kennedy won by a whisker, with some clear evidence that voter fraud in both Illinois and Texas had enabled the victory. Together with some other young Justice lawyers, I had been asked to stay late on Election Eve in the event of possible voting fraud disputes. We did receive affidavit evidence of substantial voting irregularities in Chicago as well as several rural Texas cities; but at around 3 a.m., Vice President Richard Nixon decided it would not serve the interests of the country to challenge any of the results, and we were sent home.

I had dinner occasionally with George Ofosu-Amaah, who indeed did come to work at the UN. One day, I received a long telegram from Cervenka, who was then in Accra, Ghana, working as Adviser on Atomic Energy to Kwami Nkruma, the Ghanaian head of State, inviting me to attend Ghana's World Wide Conference entitled "Ban The Bomb." All my travel and accommodation expenses would be paid by Ghana, but I had to respond rather quickly. I surmised that some other invitee had changed his mind and I was a potential replacement. From news accounts in *The New York Times*, I was aware that the Kennedy Administration strongly opposed this Conference as its theme conflicted with then U.S. foreign policy. Thus the U.S. was not sending any representatives or observers.

Strongly desiring to go, I spoke to the law firm's partners, who wisely counseled me to notify the State Department or other government entity of my invitation. They suggested not seeking U.S. government approval of my intent to go, but having their reply state that the decision was entirely mine and could not receive government approval. In this manner, they reasoned that no one could, years later, claim that I attended a Communist-supported meeting without informing the Administration, and thus imperiling political ambitions I might later have.

This seemed sensible to me so I phoned the State Department Legal Adviser's Office, where I still had friends from my work at Office of Legal Counsel. The lawyer I spoke to said he would investigate the situation and have the correct person in charge call me right away.

Amazingly, someone did call me back that afternoon, saying he was familiar with my request and had arranged for me to meet with the Assistant Secretary for African Affairs the following day at the Foggy Bottom offices of the State Department. He furnished me with the name of the official I would be meeting, his room number, and the time of my appointment.

The next morning, it was raining so I grabbed my umbrella before heading off to catch the shuttle from LaGuardia Airport. When I arrived at the designated office, the secretary quickly ushered me in to a huge oak-paneled office, as large as that of the AG's office at Justice. Two gentlemen greeted me, explained that they were aware of my interest in attending the Conference, but could not help me with a letter of any kind. Neither of the names they gave were that of the person who I had spoken to on the telephone. Their suggestion to me was that, as I had only recently left the Department of Justice, where I had worked for and been known to Nick Katzenbach, now head of my old office, one of them could send an inter-agency memo to him, explaining my request. He might return a memo, approving or having no objection to my attendance at the conference.

I pointed out, politely, that this was a pointless suggestion, as, whatever Katzenbach's confidential response to him might be, I would have no way of getting a copy of it. Thus, my interest would not be served at all. Realizing that this entire meeting was some kind of subterfuge, I ended it as quickly as I could. As I passed the secretary's desk on the way out, she stopped me, saying there was a gentleman waiting for me. This fellow, whose name I do not recall, introduced himself as the person who had spoken to me on the phone and arranged this meeting. He apologized for the tactic, but said that it was his office that was interested in my attending the conference, and could we discuss the matter over a quick lunch? I said no, but we could have a drink, as I wanted to catch the next shuttle back to New York.

We walked a block or two to the Hay-Adams Hotel bar where he confessed that his office, still unidentified, had no interest at all in what would be going on at the Conference, but was extremely anxious to keep tabs on my friend Cervenka, who they thought might be a Czech government spy; and to understand how close he was to Nkruma, what he was really up to, etc. He told me that their office would supply me with a chauffeur and car in Accra and the driver would be my local contact and helper.

"So you want me to be a spy on my friend, is that it? Even if I swallowed hard and said yes to that offensive request, I would still need that letter I told you about on the phone; so would your office give me such a letter on its stationery?"

"I can't answer that right here but I promise that I will get you an answer by tomorrow," he replied.

Back in New York City, I made phone calls to verify that, if I wanted to go, there was still time to get my required shots. I also noticed that in my haste to catch the shuttle, I had forgotten my umbrella in the hotel bar.

The following morning this fellow phoned to tell me that he could not persuade his superiors to give me the letter I wanted. I responded somewhat curtly that meant we had no further business, and was about to hang up when he said:

"By the way, you left your umbrella at the hotel yesterday and we have had it dropped off at your office."

"Thanks," I said, and hung up, hoping never to speak to this apparent CIA agent again.

I had dinner with George Ofosu-Amaah that night, because he was going home to attend the Conference and I wanted him to inform Zdenek of my efforts to attend and to express my personal appreciation for the invitation, and asked him to call me on his return so we could dine again and discuss what happened at the Conference.

George did call on his return and we had dinner at a restaurant across from UN Headquarters, where he filled me in on the conference and Zdenek's activities. The following morning, the agent who had caused my wasted trip to D.C. called me again.

"What do you want?" I impolitely asked.

"Well, it has appeared to my superiors based on what I have told them, that you would be an excellent candidate for a career with our agency, and we wanted to discuss that employment possibility with you. Also, since you had dinner with Ofosu-Amaah last night, I would like to know what he told you about Cervenka and the conference."

"So you had me tailed last night. Outrageous! Listen to me now. Probably the last outfit in the world I would work for is your Agency. I will give you no information about my discussions with George, not now or ever, and please do not contact me again."

"I'm sorry you feel that way; but should you ever

change your mind just call the number you reached me at in D.C. and we can take it from there," he replied.

And so my only real opportunity to be recruited as a CIA spook ended rather quickly, with no regret on my part.

I saw Hans Blix once or twice for lunch when he came to attend UN sessions on behalf of his government, as was also the case with Krzysz Skubiszewski, who became Poland's first post-Communist Foreign Minister. I only spoke with Owada by phone once or twice as he was stationed in D.C. on behalf of his government. Mostly, we spoke then about his lost original transcript of the lengthy paper he had written at the Centre, his failed efforts to locate it, and his having had to rewrite it. He learned painfully to always make a copy of important creations.

I did, however, have many contacts with Eli Lauterpacht over the years, several of which played peculiar roles in my later life.

Eli had many business contacts in Washington, particularly with the UN agency called ICSID. He would often telephone me from DC saying he was on his way to NYC from which he was flying home, and could we have dinner. He was always interested in keeping up with the activities of his former students. Several times I invited him to have dinner at our apartment, as I knew my then-wife,

Joan, would enjoy his humor and worldly sophistication. At one of these dinners he confirmed the rumors that I had heard that his wife had died a year after our time at the Research Centre, leaving him to raise their two children alone, with the help of nannies. He did tell me that, at the moment, he had found an Irish nanny, who appeared more competent and pleasant than any of the others.

My encounters with Eli continued over the years. I did learn that he had married the Irish nanny and they were enjoying married life together.

19

Learning to Try Cases

After leaving the Justice Department with the expectation that I would be learning how to try civil jury cases from Harold R. Tyler, who had hired me to join his then law firm, I was surprised by his abrupt departure to become a Federal District Judge. Left at the firm, I actually knew the associates and partners only slightly, never having gone through the interview process. Hoping to become a trial lawyer, I had as yet acquired none of the requisite knowledge or skills. I fully expected that I would have to re-enter the job market.

But within days the two senior partners called me into a meeting where they said they considered it fair to give me a one-year trial to see if I could learn to handle their civil litigation caseload as they usually farmed out any criminal matters that came in. They also explained that most of their civil litigation came from the General Electric Company, Rolls-Royce Engines, or the A.C. Nielsen Company. I thought they were being fair and said I would give it a try. The only reference to the partner who had hired me and then left so abruptly without any notice to any of them I now learned, was when Phil Gilbert said angrily:

"This is the second time he left us for a prettier girl, neither time giving us any warning or explanation. I don't want to hear his name mentioned to me again."

So I started being assigned whatever civil litigation existed at the firm and fortunately it was not much or very complex. After picking the brains of several of the associates whom I quickly befriended, I realized that my bible would be the New York Civil Practice Act and Rules (CPR), one volume with its pocket part, that contained all of the more arcane legal procedures that still existed in New York and which I would be endlessly using.

The cases that I started with were straightforward claims of defective appliances against the General Electric Company, sometimes coupled with the allegation that the defect had caused personal injury to the purchaser; this latter type of case had to be treated more seriously since juries often liked to award lots of money to an individual suing a large company. I researched the law carefully, spent time with the company's engineers and files, but mostly tried to slow the progress of the case toward trial. I often clashed with plaintiff's counsel in the motion parts, sometimes lost motions, but never made the same mistake twice. My hours of reading the CPR rules began to pay off as I routinely knew more of the Rules than my opponents.

At about this time, my first ever client surprisingly appeared. He was a former Washington lobbyist named Lucius Smith whom I had befriended before he moved to New York to work as a securities salesman with a large Wall Street firm. I was the only New York lawyer that he knew and he seemed to have confidence in me because of the work that I had done in Washington at the Justice Department. His case was based on an alleged "contract" that had been made between the President of the securities firm and Lucius personally, regarding commissions that would be paid to him based on the volume of shares of stock in NYSE companies that he sold. Unfortunately, the "contract" was not in writing, but he had a copy of a Memorandum on company stationery that made direct reference to his commission arrangement. My research confirmed that under the arcane provisions of the New York Statute of Frauds, the existence of the Memorandum, accompanied by credible supporting testimony, could be found by a jury to be a binding agreement allowing him to recover all of the commissions for which he was suing. So I prepared the Complaint and commenced the lawsuit for Lucius seeking what appeared in that day to be a substantial amount of money.

My time spent in the motion parts in New York County

had taught me that the backlog of commercial cases waiting to be tried was three years; only matrimonial and criminal cases received priority treatment. I had become familiar with a trick used by many crafty inhabitants of the commercial courts, which was to make an early Motion for a Temporary Injunction on some credible ground or other, argue it forcefully before a judge, and see it denied. It was then the practice of the clerks, at the direction of the judge, to place the case onto the Ready Trial Calendar for an allegedly early trial. How well it really worked in practice, I wasn't sure—or, for that matter, whether it depended on the type of case it was—but that is what I did. During this entire period, I had no one in the firm to guide me or give me advice, other than the other associates, who, it appeared, knew much less than I did.

In the interim, a passenger airliner of TACA International Airlines, propelled by four Rolls-Royce Merlin engines, had crashed on taking off from an airport in South America, resulting in large damage suits against the engine manufacturer in trial courts in both New York and New Jersey. I was pleased that Phil Gilbert assigned the defense of these cases to me, explaining that his client was not especially concerned about the money damages claimed since it was fully insured and its engines were unlikely to be found faulty. Of more concern was any possible finding that the company was subject to personal jurisdiction in the United States, which had a well-deserved reputation for subjecting companies to expensive and dangerous lawsuits of all kinds. So I was instructed to file Motions to Dismiss for Lack of Jurisdiction in both state courts. I was also called on to do elaborate research on the rapidly developing case law in that area, for it was clear that whatever was decided by the lower courts, appeals would be taken to the highest court in each state in order to resolve the jurisdictional issues. I threw myself into the assignment with enthusiasm, for the moment ignoring Lucius Smith's pending case.

But it was not entirely off my screen since the lawyer who turned up to defend the Wall Street securities firm was quite a surprise—a lower Broadway-based Jewish single practitioner, who specialized in serving me with annoying trivial motions late on a Friday afternoon with an answering date of the following Monday morning, guaranteeing my having to work over the weekend. He just did not seem to be the type of lawyer one would expect to be defending a large WASP-owned and led securities firm. When I inquired down at the courthouse about him, several clerks suggested that he was a "beard" for Milton Pollack, the dean of the class-action bar, who had terrorized many corporate management teams into large settlements of the suits he brought. In any event, I was not impressed with his kind of practice trickery. Sure enough, some weeks later, Milton Pollack's secretary was calling me on his behalf to have lunch with him at the Metropolitan Club on Fifth Avenue and 60th Street. I told her I was unavailable for lunch, which was when I often played squash, but a drink late in the day was possible, since I was curious to observe his strategy in dealing with me. We fixed the meeting for 4 p.m. the following Wednesday.

When I asked for Mr. Pollack at the entrance to his club at the appointed hour I was led by a uniformed employee to a large meeting room on its third floor, which could have held 50 people. Sitting alone at a table was a gentleman dressed in somber black with a dark blue tie. I wore my pinstriped double-breasted suit with a sprightly bow tie. We shook hands, sat opposite each other, and I ordered a coffee while Pollack continued with a martini. He explained how unhelpful my representing someone like Lucius Smith was to my otherwise promising career start as a New York City litigator. He carefully dropped enough factual details about my legal activities, teaching year at Stanford Law School, and three-year stint in the Justice Department, to convince me that some private detective agency should be indebted to me for it having received a lucrative assignment. When he dropped a reference to my recently having become a member of the Yale Club of NYC, I was certain that an agency like Pinkerton was following me about and said so. I had to hand it to Pollack for he didn't blush or miss a beat.

"Why yes, you're exactly right. And I've brought a copy of their recent report to convince you that we are serious."

"About what? I asked. "Not trying to scare me into dropping the representation I hope, for if that's what you're up to, you're going to have a quick appearance before the State Bar Ethics Committee."

"Now, now. Let's not get agitated based on a misunderstanding," said Pollack. "I am simply pointing out to you that if you read this entire report, you will see that your client does not have a history of truthfulness in his past business activities and more than likely, has not told you the entire truth about his employment arrangements with the defendant company in this case."

Interrupting, I told him we were getting nowhere; his way of dealing with me was offensive and that as far as I was concerned, our meeting was concluded. The case would continue to be handled by me and I wasn't bothered in the least by the slimy tactics of his lower Broadway front man. I did take the copy of the report he had placed on the table, got up and left as quickly and quietly as I could. The nerve of that sanctimonious, pompous egotist, I thought. Maybe that works in class action cases, but he picked the wrong boy in this case. Back to my office I went, to work on my Rolls-Royce jurisdictional research.

Sometimes you have to be careful what you ask for, when several days later my phone rang with a call from the Ready Day Calendar Clerk informing me that "The Smith case has been assigned to the Honorable Emilio Nunez for trial commencing tomorrow morning at 10:00 a.m. Please have all your witnesses ready and in the courtroom."

To me, that sounded like a death knell. I hadn't ever tried a jury case before, and only had overnight to prepare.

I rehearsed Lucius as best I could for several hours in the late afternoon and early part of the evening, and spent much of the night creating the sequence of questions necessary to introduce the sales records into evidence. I had no time to look for, or any idea how to ask about, the oral part of his contract arrangement or even the written Memorandum. At about three in the morning I took a cab home and collapsed into bed.

The next morning I met Lucius, accompanied by his

wife and two teen-age children, in front of the state courthouse in Foley Square and led them to Judge Nunez's courtroom. My creepy opponent was there, whispering to the clerks in front of the bench. The Judge soon arrived and briskly supervised the selection of six jurors. I was asked to make a brief opening statement to explain the case to the jury and outline what my client sought from them. My opponent followed with a clear short statement disputing what I had asked for. Then the judge motioned for us to approach the bench to speak to him. The first time he asked us how long we thought this case would last so he could plan the rest of his week's calendar. The second time he wanted to know what time we wished to break for lunch. We had both kept our voices very low so that no one could hear what was being discussed. These were purely administrative details.

When we were back at our respective seats he turned to me, and said politely, "Please call your first witness, Mr. Layton."

"Plaintiff calls Mr. Lucius Smith to the stand," I said, and the case was on its way.

I took Lucius through his education and business background briefly, came to his employment by the defendant corporation, and when I tried to ask about the details of the terms of his compensation in his conversation with the president of the company, my annoying opponent was on his feet in a flash with a loud "Objection!"

"Sustained," stated Judge Nunez.

I tried the same question a slightly different way.

"Same objection," shouted my learned adversary, and unfortunately, the same ruling by Judge Nunez.

I realized that the entire case was now imperiled, for if I could not get the compensation package into evidence, there was no way I could introduce the short written Memorandum, which was critical in order to satisfy the requirements of the Statute of Frauds. So I thought a bit more and tried a different approach.

"Objection," shouted Mr. Lower Broadway.

"Sustained," said Judge Nunez. I was pretty much stumped, when I saw the judge crook his forefinger toward me, signaling that I should approach the bench, which I started doing, as did Mr. Lower Broadway. But the judge quickly shook his head signaling him to sit down. When I got before the judge he spoke to me in a very low voice.

"Is this your first jury trial?"

"Yes, your Honor."

"I thought so," he said. "You're doing terribly. But I can't let your client, and that nice family that I see with him, suffer because of your incompetence. He is obviously owed a lot of money. Do you have a pen and something to write on with you?"

"Yes, Your Honor."

"Well, copy this down exactly as I dictate it and that is what you will ask him when you resume questioning him. Exactly as I told you. Now get back there."

Humbled and immensely relieved, I put the question, exactly as dictated by the judge, to Lucius.

"Objection!" came the voice from the other side of the room.

"Overruled," responded Judge Nunez, and said to the witness, "You may answer."

Out poured Lucius' many-times rehearsed recital of his oral agreement with the president as to his commission earnings, and I was able to offer the Memorandum into evidence, where it was received—over Lower Broadway's somewhat muted objection. A minute or so later the Clerk announced that we would be taking our noon recess and that everyone must be back by 1:30 p.m. I saw my little opponent scurry out of the courtroom to a telephone kiosk across the hall, no doubt to take instruction from the great Milton Pollack. Sure enough, while Lucius, his wife, and sons, and I were gathering our coats and briefcases and court papers to work with over lunch, Lower Broadway raced back into the room and signaled me that he wanted to talk. When I went over to him, he agitatedly offered me a handsome sum of money to settle the case right then, so that there would be no afternoon session, no jury verdict, and no press coverage the following day. I bargained a bit, and spoke to the Smiths, who happily agreed to a $75,000 settlement, which was more than they had hoped for.

We had a very relaxed lunch and I returned to the Courtroom. My opponent and I told Judge Nunez of the settlement and placed it on the record with the Court Reporter. Obviously pleased, Judge Nunez thanked both of us for our good judgment in settling. I thanked him for "all of his courtesies" and left.

Lucius had invited us all to a celebratory dinner on him at a good midtown restaurant where his family and some of his colleagues would be present. Toward the end of the dinner, much wine and alcohol having been consumed, I heard a clinking of fork on glass and saw Lucius get up to make a speech.

"This is a toast," he declared. "To my lawyer, Bob Layton, the best lawyer in the City of New York. Those of you who watched him in the trial saw that while at first Judge Nunez was talking to both of them up at his bench, but after a while, he would only talk to my lawyer! Now a toast! All of you—to the best lawyer in New York—Bob Layton!" I said not a word but I did have a private chuckle and then, a great night's sleep.

After the Smith case, I was assigned to defend the Rolls-Royce Motor Car Company, rather than its Engine Division, in a case claiming $2 million in damages by a disgruntled millionaire-owner of two Rolls-Royce sedans that he claimed were defectively designed and manufactured. His chauffeur was his principal witness but I called the owner to the stand for questioning before the jury, since I had said in my opening that the case could be summed up by asking:

"Was the problem with these cars the nuts that held the wheels on—or rather the nut behind the wheel?"

I knew the owner was arrogant and liked to display his wealth, and the jury liked him no better than the company engineers did when he berated them in front of their superiors. The jury took only an hour to return a verdict for the defendant on a late Friday afternoon, allowing me to call the senior partner with the good news in time to transmit it to the Company officials.

{A footnote, on behalf of truth—not always a feature in jury trials—is appropriate. Wealthy purchasers of Rolls-

Royce motor cars in the USA were cautioned not to buy them if their use would involve crowded city driving—such as in Manhattan. The cars were principally designed for use on English country roads. Some years later, this problem was solved by devices that kept the British engines from overheating in city driving and to stop running.}

I was soon back to the South American air crash case I'd previously been working on. After a year of heavy motion practice in New York State Supreme Court as well as in New Jersey State Court, where we located excellent local counsel, I was admitted for the purpose of arguing these technical jurisdiction motions *pro hac vice* (for this case only). I thought my arguments in both courts went very well. We had to wait several months for the written decisions but were very pleased when we won both of them.

The law firm for TACA airlines then decided to appeal from the New York decision only, and to drop the New Jersey case. Once again, I was asked to handle that appeal entirely on my own, thus demonstrating to me that I had convinced the law firm of my ability to try cases and argue appeals.

20

My Short, Disastrous Career
as a Criminal Lawyer

At the conclusion of my three-year stint at the Department of Justice, I had accepted an offer from the departing head of the Civil Rights Division to join his law firm in New York City where he had promised to teach me how to become a skilled court room professional. The firm was midsized for New York City, located in the midtown area. It had both an excellent reputation and an impressive roster of corporate clients. Then, less than three months after my joining, I learned, one bright morning, from the buzz of gossip among the other associates and secretaries that my mentor had accepted an offer from the Kennedy administration to become a federal district judge and was already testifying at his confirmation hearing in Washington that morning. Thus, I was left untrained and without the first clue as to how to try any kind of case— civil or criminal.

Several weeks after he was sworn in as a district judge, he did phone me saying he'd given my name to three sitting fellow judges at the Southern District Courthouse for a possible assignment as unpaid counsel to indigent criminal defendants as there were, at that time, no provisions for providing counsel to poor persons accused of a federal crime.

"Why did you do that?" I asked.

"Well, you're young and could use the training", he responded.

I restrained myself and simply said, "Thanks a lot."

I then went to the senior partner of the firm and asked him what I should do, since I had already been assigned a boatload of civil casework for paying clients of the firm.

"Well, you can't say no to federal judges. This will get you some good experience and put us in good favor with three sitting judges. I'll transfer some of your work to other associates. Good luck."

Sure enough, the phone rang the next morning with a call from the first judge—a case of alleged theft of a Social Security check from an elderly person's apartment house mailbox. I quickly chatted with one of my fellow associates, who had been an Assistant U.S. Attorney in the criminal division in that courthouse and was told by him in a three-minute briefing that in most of these assigned criminal cases, the defendants are guilty and are willing to plead that way if you are able to negotiate a lower sentence with the government prosecutor. So, several days later, I took the subway to the courthouse, read the file, made copies for myself, and then made an appointment to meet with my first criminal client in a coffee shop nearby as he was out on bail, having had no prior criminal record. He turned out to be more than willing to plead guilty if I could get him a suspended sentence—or a very short jail term. The government lawyer was pleasant, cooperative, and we worked out a suspended sentence in return for the guilty plea. Case #1 done!

The second judge's call came within days and was also not too much of a problem since it had similar facts, but my client had forged the endorsement on a stolen Social Security check and had a prior record. So, the negotiation was much more difficult and the guilty plea had to result in a one-year jail term. Still, no trial experience. Then came case #3, for which I was totally unprepared.

I was introduced to my third client, a Mr. Robert Baggett, in the holding cells of the Federal Detention Center in the basement of the Federal Courthouse in Foley Square. Baggett, I learned, was one of three black men accused of stealing a large quantity of expensive leather suitcases, cases of liquor, boxes of imported Havana cigars, and designer clothes from the Railway Express Terminal at 11th Avenue and 38th Street in Manhattan. All three were apprehended on the premises late at night in possession of the missing goods. But the other two, Baggett informed me, were out on $5000 bail, which they had been able to put up, and had a lawyer of their own, who they claimed to have paid. So, I was the only unpaid counsel and my man was in the slammer. I inquired why that was the case. Baggett said the government wouldn't consider bail for him since he was from out of town; he lived, he said, in some small town in South Carolina. That didn't make complete sense to me, so I inquired whether he had any prior convictions. "No sir, not a one!" I should mention that he was about 6'3" tall and easily weighed 225 pounds, with the appearance of either a boxer or professional wrestler.

I told him that I wanted to try to get him out on bail, mostly because I didn't want to keep meeting him in the holding cells, and thought it was worth the trouble of making a bail motion for my own convenience as well as Baggett's. So, I told him I would be back the next day with one of my sport jackets along with a shirt and tie, since he would have to appear in court with me for the bail application; he could keep the borrowed clothes for the trial as well, since juries always, or so I had been told, like to see defendants dressed neatly. He seemed to understand everything I said. Before I left, I asked again about any prior convictions. "No sir," he repeated.

It took me several days to prepare the motion for bail, copying from formbooks, and asking questions of other associates. The motion came before Judge John M. Canella, who appeared to be an extremely polite, considerate man as I listened to the argument of motions that were heard before Baggett's. He had been brought up by elevator from the holding cells by the guards and was sitting beside me, wearing the borrowed clothes, as we waited our turn. Eventually, the clerk called "*United States of America v. Robert Baggett*" and I was on my feet.

The judge said politely that he had read my affidavit and brief and thought that it made a case for the awarding of bail and asked opposing counsel for a response.

The Assistant U.S. Attorney was quick to say, "Well, your honor, Mr. Layton is correct in saying that his client, Mr. Baggett, has no prior convictions under that name, but the government is prepared to hand up certified copies of his prior convictions for robbery under the name Slaggett in North Carolina, under the name Taggett for theft from a Railway Express Agency in Georgia, and for attempted robbery under the name Claggett in his home state of South Carolina."

I wished that a hole would have opened in the floor

under me and permitted my escape from that courtroom but I was relieved to hear the judge say, "Well, I am certain that Mr. Layton was unaware of these prior convictions; but under the circumstances, I must deny your motion, Mr. Layton. The guards will return the prisoner. Next case."

I glared at Baggett with disdain but he wouldn't look me in the eye. During the following weeks, I tried as best I could to investigate the facts as alleged in the government indictment by journeying to Harlem and asking questions not only about Baggett but about his two co-defendants who were out on bail, and their defense lawyer, whose name was William T. Chance. I interviewed the guards on duty at the REA offices on the night of the robbery, and I read the spots off the affidavit of the FBI agent who obviously was going to be the government's principal witness. I was forced to spend a lot of the law firm's time on Mr. Baggett. The time for trial was fixed for early December and I met with Baggett on several occasions and thought I was ready. On the morning of the trial, I was surprised to find that my co-counsel, William Chance, was nowhere to be seen. The judge who turned up on the bench was none other than Judge Lloyd McMahon, whose reputation for fierceness, harsh sentences to criminal defendants, and rudeness to counsel was well known throughout the courthouse. After a while, the judge called for the jury panel to be brought in. Around that time, a middle-aged black man in a well-tailored suit came in and sat down beside me.

"Mr. Layton? I am Bill Chance."

"Nice to meet you. Do you want to question the prospective jurors first since you're senior to me and your clients are named first in the indictment?"

"No thanks," he said. "You just go ahead and ask all the questions. I don't have any."

That's the way it went throughout the entire trial, which took all of two days, with Chance never asking one question of anybody. During the lunch recess I went up to the court clerk and asked him in a whisper, "What is it with my co-counsel? He shows up late and never speaks."

"Don't you know about him? I thought everybody knows about 'Last Clear Chance'!"

"Is that what he's called?"

"Yup, and it's accurate. Hiring him is like a guaranteed ticket to the slammer."

"But why do people hire him?"

"Beats me," said the clerk.

The case ended late in the second day, after I had tried my hand at cross-examination of the government's principal witness, the FBI agent. Actually, I did not do too badly, after all the investigating I had done, tripping him up on some of the facts alleged in his affidavit prepared by his government counsel. After arguments to the jury, Mr. Chance said I was speaking for him as well, and after the government's closing, Judge McMahon gave a relatively fair charge to the jury, and he sent them out to deliberate at about 5 o'clock, apparently thinking they would be back before dinner time, so they could get home for dinner. That didn't happen. At 7 p.m., they were called in for a report and the foreman reported that they were deadlocked. The judge was obviously miffed. So, he gave them another charge, called, I later learned, an *Allen* charge, from an old case where a jury was deadlocked for several days. An *Allen* charge almost directly instructs the jury to convict for the sake of everybody involved. I was upset but could do nothing. They were sent out to a restaurant on the government's tab along with two Federal marshals. Back they came at 10:30 p.m., deadlocked again. McMahon looked furious and he then gave them another *Allen* charge, sprucing it up with some direct language. They went out again, returning with a guilty verdict at midnight. I was very upset, told Baggett I would see him at the sentencing, which was set for four weeks away, and trudged home.

On the day of sentencing I got up early to practice my speech in mitigation of Baggett's sentence in front of my bathroom mirror. It was 20 minutes long. On arrival at the courtroom, I was shocked to find that the two co-defendants represented by Mr. Chance were not present, and the bailiff reported that they jumped bail and were being pursued by the FBI. Chance was also a no-show.

I thought this would surely put McMahon in a great frame of mind for sentencing my client. He quickly asked me if I had anything to say. I stood up, cleared my throat, and started my prepared speech. He interrupted me immediately.

"No, no. I have heard hundreds of those. Just answer one question. Is this the case where the jury was deadlocked until midnight?"

"Yes, Your Honor."

"That's all I need to know. Based on the fact that the jury had some doubts about the guilt of the defendant, I impose a sentence of six months. Next case."

I went down in the elevator with Baggett in order to recover my jacket, shirt and tie and while he was removing them and handing them back to me, I told him how badly I felt about the result and that I would have a Notice of Appeal filed by the next afternoon in hopes of getting the conviction reversed. He looked at me as though I were crazy, handed me the last of my borrowed clothing and then, towering over me, he reached down and grabbed me by the shirt collar and tie, raising me several inches off the ground and said in a loud, clear voice: "Listen here white boy! You don't do nothin' of the kind! I can do six months standing on my head and I don't need you to screw it up now!"

He put me down, turned away and left the elevator, leaving me standing in shock.

As the elevator returned me to the first floor and I staggered down the courthouse steps toward the subway entrance, I vowed to myself that, "Enough is enough. My career at the criminal bar is now over." And so it was, and the better for all concerned.

21

The Nielsen Television Ratings Chase

In the mid-sixties the Nielsen Television ratings were the golden markers of success. Most viewers did not know that the statistical sample used was only approximately 1,400 houses where the families had agreed to allow a small box to be attached to their TV set, which would record their viewing choices. They received $5 each month for agreeing to be part of the national sample. A Congressional committee had held hearings on the manner by which Nielsen came up with its ratings only six months earlier, and now the Company was concerned that someone was trying to tamper with its ratings. My firm represented the A.C. Nielsen Company in NYC, although it had never had any litigation assignments until now. Harold Segall had represented them for years, but the client was not a major one for the firm.

One day Segall called me into his office and told me that the tampering issue could be a breakthrough assignment for our firm as most of the lucrative Nielsen work was done in Chicago by Sidley & Austin, a large Chicago firm. However, New York was the headquarters of the TV business. Moreover, the Company had learned that a strange survey was being mailed out from a brownstone building on East 33rd Street to each of the 1,400 TV set owners in the Nielsen sample.

I asked for a copy of the survey as well as a list from Nielsen of the names of all who might have any interest in influencing, or tampering with, the sample. I then prepared a short affidavit for each of the many persons named on the Nielsen list. The affidavit stated that they had nothing at all to do with any tampering with the Nielsen National sample. I then asked each of the named persons to read and then sign the affidavit before a Notary. My idea was that, when we discovered the guilty party or parties, we would be one step ahead because they would already be guilty of perjury. Then we would only have to nail them with whatever state or federal crimes that had been committed, to say nothing of the civil damages for which they might be liable.

Harold liked all of this but said the company was somewhat nervous since a lot of important names were on the list they had prepared. I pointed out that the company retained the right to enforce or not enforce all or part of its rights. So we went ahead and got signatures on all of the affidavits. Some of the signers were big show business names.

Meanwhile, I hired a private detective to learn which of

the tenants in the 33rd Street brownstone was mailing out the surveys, and receiving the responses. The detective mailed a bright red envelope to the apartment number of the tenant who sent out the survey and then used a high magnification telescope from across the street to watch the opening of the hallway mailboxes each morning. When he saw who collected the bright red envelope, he chatted with some of the other tenants and learned the name of the tenant, and we had our co-conspirator, so to speak. I then served a motion to take a deposition in aid of bringing a Complaint, a little used section of the CPLR I had used once before, and had the motion papers served on Mr. McArthur, who we now knew resided in the apartment belonging to the mailbox.

On the morning of the deposition, which I had arranged to take place in Mr. McArthur's walk-up apartment, two obviously highly paid lawyers turned up, claiming to represent him. I was more than suspicious. As soon as I asked my first question, one of them objected on the grounds of possible self-incrimination. They then notified me that they would so object to each and every question I would ask so there was little point to continuing, and I could seek a ruling from a judge if I cared to do so.

I ignored them, turned to Mr. McArthur and said to

him, "I doubt these are lawyers whom you hired and are going to pay. They are obviously hired guns paid by someone who is behind this survey scheme and who rented your mailbox for a small fee. They are not going to look out for your rights. Think it over, and consider how you might be best protected. I'll be back tomorrow morning, same time, and I have only one question for you—the name, address and phone number of the person who rented your box and how much you were paid. That's it; over and done with. But that's what these two bozos are hired to prevent. So sleep on it, Mr. McArthur."

The following morning I was back, as was everybody else. As we started, Mr. McArthur said that he was not represented by counsel; I should ask my questions and he would answer without invoking any Fifth Amendment rights. When I asked who paid him to mail out 1,400 questionnaires he replied, "Mr. Rex Sparger."

"And how much did he pay you?" I asked.

"Three hundred dollars," came the answer.

"Please tell us his address and phone number," I said.

"I only know he called me from Tulsa, Oklahoma. I never got a phone number or address."

"That concludes my questions, gentlemen. Your witness."

The hired guns sputtered some, but they had no questions, and the first part of my job was done.

I consulted with Harold and the Nielsen Company VP who was handling this for his company, and learned that Mr. Sparger had been one of the staff members of the Congressional Committee that had conducted hearings into the TV ratings industry; Sparger probably had access to the confidentially submitted list of 1,400 Nielsen viewers. That could certainly get him into a lot of trouble, but it did not explain the purpose of the scheme: specifically, who was paying him and why? We reviewed the names of those who had been asked to sign the affidavits to see if that would shed any light, but nothing jumped out. So we concluded that I had to go to Tulsa to solve the last part of the puzzle. Meanwhile, in *The New York Times* each day, the TV critic Jack Gould was having a field day criticizing the Nielsen Company and its small statistical sampling technique.

I stopped off in Chicago to meet with one of the Sidley & Austin lawyers who I knew well. Since he had grown up in Tulsa, he had some local Tulsa counsel names, and I was able to pick his brain as well. Then it was on to Tulsa, where I contacted the local counsel recommended to me and looked up Mr. Sparger in the local phone directory.

I had learned from my local counsel the name of the

bank most businessmen used and went there. Using the name of my local counsel as an introduction, I got the head teller, a bright woman, to tell me straight off that Mr. Sparger was a good customer of the bank and had worked for a Congressional Committee last year. I engaged her in more local chitchat, leading up to my principal question:

"Has Mr. Sparger been depositing large checks into his savings account recently?"

She gulped and said that it was not appropriate for her to answer that kind of question, which was absolutely true. I then explained that the local counsel and I were investigating Mr. Sparger for the Congressional Committee that Sparger had worked for, since he had misused some confidential information turned over to the Committee. This seemed to mollify her and she said only that he had been depositing some large checks drawn on a Chicago bank.

"Can you tell me whose checks these were?" I asked.

"I'll have to sleep on that one, Mr. Layton. I don't want to get into trouble."

"I understand completely", I said. "I'll be back tomorrow to see what you think."

I left the bank and headed back to confer with my local counsel. After discussing the situation at length, this lawyer said that he knew the head teller well enough to phone her at home that night, and he thought he could persuade her to give the name of the payer of the checks to him. So I left it that way. He phoned me at my hotel early the next day and told me to go over to the bank to see her again and get the information. When I got to the bank, the teller handed me a slip of paper with a name on it, and told me that she believed Rex Sparger was up to no good. I thanked her profusely and hurried back to my hotel room to examine the list of names we had gotten sworn affidavits from, because, Charles Lowe, the name on the slip of paper, meant nothing to me. But when I read the list again it became crystal clear: the name was that of Carol Channing's husband/manager, Charles Lowe. Carol Channing had enjoyed a successful career in the theatre and her husband did not want to lose out on the windfall sums being made from television.

I also recalled that on the last page of the survey mailed to the Nielsen 1,400 were several questions about whether the viewer planned to watch the upcoming new show, *An Evening with Carol Channing*, scheduled to make its opening performance within the next two weeks. If the viewer actually saw the show, he could receive by mail a $5 payment from the A.C. Nielsen Company!

I then called Segall in New York with the news regarding Carol Channing and her husband, explaining that,

223

with their signed affidavits and proof of payments to Rex Sparger, they would be sitting ducks in a large damage suit brought by the Nielsen Company against them. I told him I could start drafting the complaint on the return flight from Tulsa. He advised holding off doing anything until he had spoken with the Nielsen people in charge of this situation.

"Just make your plane reservation and come on back here. That's a job well done," he told me.

It shouldn't be a big surprise that the Nielsen people did nothing about the entire scam. Having learned why their sacred 1,400 National Sample had been tampered with, and assured of its non-recurrence (by a tactful exchange of letters between Sidley & Austin and counsel for Ms. Channing and her husband), the Nielsen execs felt that the publicity accompanying the lawsuit was not desirable.

"Tell Layton he did a good job, but we don't want to feed the gossip columns and Jack Gould with any more ammunition than they already have."

So I flew home and never even bothered to watch *An Evening With Carol Channing* on television. It did probably garner a rating higher than it deserved and her star status survived it all. I went back to taking care of my less interesting cases.

22

The Kennedy Assassination and the Warren Commission

After I left Washington and the government, I continued an involvement I had with the American Bar Association as the Secretary of its Section of International and Comparative Law, a task which I could perform equally as well from my new location in New York. The advancement practice was to complete several years as Secretary, then move to chair one of its Divisions, then to Chairman-Elect, and eventually to the hallowed year as Chair of the entire Section. I had just recently been asked to serve as Secretary.

On November 22, 1963, a date that many Americans can never forget, I was hosting with others a meeting of the Section at The Lawyers Club located on lower Broadway, at which we were having a distinguished professor of comparative law from Columbia Law School whom I had invited as our speaker. Several minutes after I had introduced him and he began his talk on Soviet law, a gentleman from the Club staff rushed to the podium to interrupt our speaker and announce in a frightened voice:

"President Kennedy has been shot in Dallas and appears

to be in very serious condition at the local hospital there."

The meeting ended, with everyone scrambling for the exits and telephones, or simply rushing back to their offices. I mumbled some words of apology to our guest, and made for the subway uptown as well. Everyone that I knew was stunned, depressed, and mystified at how such a senseless event could take place in the United States. The gunning down of the purported assassin as well as his killer, in the days following did nothing to lighten the depression that many young people experienced for a long period thereafter.

Approximately a week later, a friend from the Solicitor General's Office at Justice, Rick Medalie, phoned to tell me that Mr. Rankin, former Solicitor General and his old boss, who had been appointed as a member of the Warren Commission, was charged with hiring an investigative staff, that he had been so appointed, and was now recommending me to Rankin. He explained some of the details of the job, its tenure, which was estimated at approximately two years, and asked me to think about it, and call him back in a couple of days as they were under some time pressure. He, of course, said it would be wonderful to be working together, especially on such an important task.

When I hung up I started thinking hard. Yes it was true

that President Johnson's creation of the Warren Commission was front-page news every day; each new member appointed was analyzed and scrutinized in the pages of *The New York Times*, *Washington Post*, etc. Still, there were some very strange appointees, and most of them very political, in my view. Many commentators had suggested that it was going to be a cover-up of whatever had taken place, with no serious interest in probing deeply into how these strange events had occurred.

In other words, there would be a hasty confirmation of the lone assassin theory, then, onto more important matters. I spoke with friends with more political savvy than I had, as well as two of the older partners in my law firm, Gilbert and Segall. They were quite blunt in stating that while it sounded exciting at first, that they had no way of guaranteeing to me that there would be a vacancy for me at the firm should I care to return after the Commission's Report was done. That thought pretty much nailed it for me, as I realized that this was a risk not lightly to be taken. For the Commission members or people like Rick who intended to continue careers in government, or at least certainly living in D.C., the risk was much less. Leaving New York and a job that I had been excelling at, was taking more of a gamble than I was prepared for. I called Rick back to thank him greatly for his recommendation, sent my best wishes to Mr. Rankin, whom I knew only slightly, but politely declined the offer. I have never regretted my decision.

The history of the Warren Commission is a mixed bag. Much criticism has been leveled at its report, from both sides and many points of view. But there is little doubt that its single bullet theory and inability to account for other inconsistencies have left it as a modestly respected effort, and in my view nothing good seemed to befall any of its staff members upon the completion of their assignments.

23

The Legality of the U.S. Legal Position in Vietnam and the ABA

Following the outbreak of hostilities in Vietnam between the armed forces in the North and South, disagreement erupted in the United States concerning the legitimacy of American involvement in those hostilities. At the time I was a member of the Committee on International Law of the Association of the Bar of New York City, chaired by Carlisle E. Maw, a senior partner in the prestigious firm of Cravath, Swaine & Moore. He appointed me, along with Elliot E. Hawkins, another younger member, to a subcommittee chaired by William R. Everdell, a senior partner in another major Wall Street firm. We were to write a report on the legal position of the United States in the Vietnamese hostilities. A major impetus for appointment of the subcommittee was the almost daily attack launched against the U.S. involvement by Senator Wayne Morse of Oregon on the floor of the U.S. Senate.

At the first meeting of the subcommittee in Mr. Everdell's office, he disclosed that he was going to have a hard time signing any report that supported Morse's views as he had a son serving as a Marine Lieutenant in Vietnam. Elliott and I spent some two weeks in the City Bar library before coming up with our draft that found no credible support for the U.S. involvement. Mr. Everdell expressed his skepticism as to our conclusions, but said he would check the draft thoroughly via his own research, and then informed us that he was persuaded that we were correct and signed it to make it unanimous. The report was reviewed by the full Committee, and then by the Executive Committee of the Association, and then transmitted to the White House and the State Department Legal Adviser's Office.

Entirely unconnected from that activity, I was still Secretary of the Section of International & Comparative Law of the ABA Section. One of my duties there was to prepare the Agenda for the mid-year meeting of the Section in Chicago in December 1966, which I did based on long-standing arrangements approved by the Section Officers and mailed out to all expected attendees at the mid-year meeting. At 9 o'clock on the Sunday morning of that meeting of the Council, I noticed a flurry of activity among the older Officers and several long-time members. They were conferring with a member of the staff of Sen. Russell B. Long of Louisiana, as I learned when they called me over. They wanted an emergency addition to the Agenda—

a resolution from the Council, proposed by Senator Long, which, in effect, would declare that the U.S. military involvement in Vietnam was legal, based on a lengthy study and Report of the Section. I objected that the Section rules fixed the Agenda months in advance of the meeting. Moreover, I was aware of no study undertaken by any Section committee on the subject of Vietnam. They responded, "We'll see about that at the meeting."

After asking me to call the roll, the Chair told the assembled group that Sen. Russell Long wished to introduce a motion to adopt an emergency resolution on the legality of the conflict in Vietnam and asked for approval by the Council to add that item to the Agenda as a matter of national importance. I noted that such a motion was out of order under the long-standing rules of the Section, that no study of the subject had been made, and that such a matter could not go forward except by a unanimous vote of all members in attendance.

"Very well," snapped the Chair, "We will have a vote. All those in favor of adding the Long motion to the Agenda as a matter of the most immediate urgency, signify by saying 'Aye'. And those opposed, signify by saying 'Nay'."

I said 'Nay'. The vote was recorded by my announcing: nine Ayes and 1 Nay, for a result of passage by 9 to 1.

The discussion that took place was brief in the extreme and loaded with criticism of Senator Morse. It concluded by appointing a sub-committee on the spot to confer with Dean Erwin N. Griswold of the Harvard Law School, who was our Section representative to the House of Delegates of the ABA. The House of Delegates was in session that day in the Grand Ballroom of the Chicago hotel where all these events took place, and my colleagues wanted Griswold to introduce their Resolution and have it adopted by the ABA that very day. The members of the subcommittee departed immediately to perform their task, and I remained to see to the remaining Agenda items with the Chair and other members still present. At the conclusion of the meeting I made certain to preserve my handwritten notes. Then, I sauntered across the hall to the Grand Ballroom, where I observed the subcommittee members ringed around Dean Griswold. I felt sympathetic to Griswold who was being taken for a ride by Russell Long's people. There was much consternation when no one could put their hands on a copy of the alleged in-depth study of the legality issue allegedly made by one of the Section's committees. Since this was no concern of mine and was not part of my duties, I proceeded to check out of the Chicago hotel and headed to the airport for my return flight to Manhattan. When I read Monday's

New York Times I was amazed to see a three-column headline blaring the news that the prestigious American Bar Association had passed a resolution fully endorsing the Johnson Administration's position on the Vietnamese conflict against the legal claims of Senator Wayne Morse. As I read further, I came across the statement that the resolution emanated from my Section, where it had been unanimously passed following a lengthy study of the legal issues raised by applicable treaties and UN Resolutions. I shook my head and went to my office determined to forget about the unpleasant result of yesterday's meetings, and remembering once again why I had little interest in ever being a politician. I felt a little sorry for Griswold, but it was not my job to straighten it out, and my Section superiors would strongly disapprove if I tried.

However, the following morning brought stirrings of real trouble. The *New York Times* printed a Letter to the Editor by Harvard Law School professor, Jerome A. Cohen, who had graduated from Yale Law School a year ahead of me, whom I knew, and who had been selected as the first U.S. lawyer-recipient of a Ford Foundation scholarship to study Japanese intensively for five years. Jerry's letter started out by calling the ABA lots of names, all on the theme of it being no different than the legal toadies of the

Communist Chinese or the Soviet Union and other dictatorships. He attacked any claim that the ABA may have acted independently of political interest. I hoped that the ABA crew would let Cohen's letter pass but they didn't.

On Tuesday came a response in the *New York Times* by one of their lesser-known Section members, a Mr. Ben Busch, who was on the Council that "unanimously" passed the controversial resolution, and who knowingly putting his name to the lie about the lengthy legal study. I was aware that he had served with distinction in World War II, as a member of the Alpine Ski Troops, which were well thought of, so he was being fronted, as a combat veteran, in an all-out effort to cover up the Council's rampant misconduct. This was all in the desperate hope that the truth would never come to the attention of Dean Griswold, who had apparently swallowed their story in its entirety.

But Busch's letter was too much for me to bear. It repeatedly referred to the lengthy, thorough, (but non-existent) legal study of some six months duration; the unanimous vote of the Council of the Section; the thorough debate among the Council members prior to their vote, etc. Deciding to call Jerry Cohen in order to tell him the truth, I knew that my career at the ABA would be over. I never really thought of myself as a bar association careerist. For me it was always the subject matter, which I had been interested in since working for Professor McDougal. I was completely happy with my Committee work at the City Bar Association, whose members I truly respected. Let the ABA kick me out; I would find it a relief. There goes another line on the résumé!

I was planning to get married that April and since the Annual Meeting of the ABA that year was scheduled to take place in August in Honolulu, Hawaii, we had planned to delay our honeymoon until the ABA Meeting. We would then stay on in Maui for a week, where my law school roommate Chuck Ames owned what he described as a lovely condo on the beach that he was making available as a wedding gift. I knew the Section moguls would quietly drop me from their slate, and I didn't care one bit. I prepared my bride, who was quite pleased, as she said that she had met some boring lawyers and their wives before (her father and brother were both lawyers) but my ABA colleagues were some of the dullest and most uninteresting she had ever met.

All this is by way of background to what happened to my too clever by far Section big shots. I reached Jerry Cohen at his office at the Harvard Law School the day following the appearance of Busch's Letter to the Editor in the *New York Times*. When I told him that I knew the vote was not unanimous, because as Secretary of the Council, I had the job of recording my own dissent, he started howling with glee. I then told him that not only was there no study at all, but that these morons didn't know the difference between the SEATO Treaty and the *Declaration of Independence*, that they never thought for a moment about the legal basis of the U.S. involvement, and that they had obviously conspired not only to lie to Griswold, but to put Busch up to making Jerry look as bad as possible. Jerry had stopped laughing. He asked if he could have my permission to explain these facts to his Dean, whose office was down the hall. I replied that I wouldn't have placed my call without having decided that one in advance—and that the answer was yes. He explained that there were going to be some serious fireworks because Griswold was the loveliest and the most gentle of souls, besides being a brilliant scholar and lawyer. But once he had been lied to, he erupted—something like Mount Vesuvius, said Jerry. I replied that I had fully thought out the consequences to myself and I didn't care what they did to me. But I was not going to sit by and see them get away with this assemblage of lies. I told him it was OK with me if Griswold was turned loose.

A couple of days later Jerry phoned me to report that after Dean Griswold calmed down, he arranged for the entire leadership group of the Section of International and Comparative Law (absent me) to fly out to Chicago with him, where they met with the top honchos of the ABA. The result was that the Section's ability to propose or introduce resolutions was taken away from them for three years, and that a trusteeship was imposed on them. Busch was made to write a letter of apology to Cohen, who said that my name did not come up at all. Griswold never forgave any of them for having taken advantage of his good faith.

Many years later, Dean Griswold and I became partners in the same very large (Jones Day) law firm; I had need of a skilled appellate advocate with an academic pedigree for the Guess/Jordache blue jeans litigation in a California Appellate Court, and I reached out to Griswold, asking that he fly out to L.A. to argue our case. He agreed, did a fabulous job, and won the appeal. I reminded him of the ABA incident when I picked him up at the airport. Of course, he hadn't known of my involvement then, but he was very gracious and said he couldn't stay angry with those Section politicians, but that they had set new standards for skullduggery.

Some years later, I had gotten divorced from my first

wife and married a charming French woman I had met in the French Government's Trade Office in New York City. We continued my practice of being weekenders in the small Northwestern Connecticut community of Lakeville, where we found quite a handsome French-style old estate in a section of the town that was unfamiliar to me. It turned out that our neighbor to the south of us was a lady named Phyllis Busch, and we became quite friendly with her. One Saturday afternoon when we were having tea in her house, the discussion turned to what I did for a living. When I admitted that I was a lawyer, specializing in international litigation, she said that perhaps I had known her husband, Benjamin Busch, who practiced in that field, but had passed away several years earlier. As I did not wish to explain the fracas before the ABA, I simply replied that I knew of him, but we had not worked together on any matter to my recollection. Some time later, after it became clear that she and Busch were not happily married, I told her of the ABA incident and she responded by saying that his conduct did not surprise her.

24

Going on My Own

By 1972, I had almost eleven years of experience as a litigator, or trial lawyer, in what, for those times, was known as a medium-sized, midtown New York City law firm. I had been there as an associate since leaving the Justice Department hoping to become a partner in the firm. I was still a bachelor casting about for someone I might fall in love with and marry, when of all things, the senior partner of the firm, Phil Gilbert, began dropping in to my office at the close of the business day and opening the conversation by casually asking if I had a "hot date" set up for that evening. Irrespective of whether I did have a date or not, I replied that I didn't, and he then asked me to have a drink with him.

The first time or two that this happened I thought that his wife must be away and he was lonely, but after he began to put away three to four martinis and getting a bit drunk, it became clear that it was his lack of a true marriage that was the problem. Like most married men with a family he lived in the suburbs of Westchester and commuted to and from Manhattan each day. He took to talking to me about his broken marriage, never asked to have dinner with me, and ultimately needed me to pour him into a taxi headed to Grand Central Station to catch his commuter train to the suburbs. While at first, we did our drinking at Madison Avenue hotel bars, he seemed aware that I lived near our office and suggested that we could relax more in the privacy of my apartment. I readily agreed as he began drinking more than was seemly in public and I stood the cost of his martinis with ease and sipped one drink slowly most of these evenings.

"You won't believe what she's up to now. Seeing a psychiatrist about me, mostly, and of all things—a Freudian, the worst kind, you know. They never let go!"

I commiserated with him as best I could, pretending that I was aware of the perils of Freudian therapy treatment, which, in actuality, I knew not a thing about.

"When I married her, she was a pretty little thing just out of Smith from a wealthy Chicago family and I had already graduated from Andover and Dartmouth, served two years in the Army as a Second Lieutenant in WWII, and was graduating from Harvard Law School with first class grades. We've got two grown kids now, a big house, and I'm being cut apart by some Jewish disciple of Sigmund Freud. Where's the fairness in any of this?"

I, along with three other associates, had been made

partner by the two founders of the firm, not because we were all outstanding lawyers but, it appeared to me, because otherwise we might each leave, since other firms were growing and it had become common practice to lure talent away from firms that were underpaying their lawyers, which mine was certainly doing.

While I had begun to attract some clients (such as the Lucius Smith case earlier described) and had accepted the partnership "promotion", I had already decided that if my firm did not start to open up, hire real talent, which could only be done by paying for it, that somehow, I would find a way to leave. After all, there was still linoleum covering its floors instead of carpets, despite the firm's Park Avenue address. Ultimately, the break with the firm came under peculiar circumstances.

On a day late in June 1972, my phone rang and it was one of my law school classmates whose last name started with "L" and thus, we sat near each other in several classes as his name was Everett "Skip" Lowe. Not having spoken to him since our graduation in May 1954, I was curious as to why he was calling. His story was that he was now part of a corporate management group led by a business executive named Jack Vollbrecht, which had been running Dresser Industries, a large conglomerate located in

Houston, Texas. The entire group had been fired summarily when its business took a downturn.

"Right now, I'm trying to support my wife and kids by practicing law from my bedroom," said Everett. "I have only one client and he and his corporation have just been sued in the Supreme Court of the State of New York, County of New York, and you're the only one from our class who I know who practices in New York, and I hope you do litigation; so can you help me? I'll eventually be able to pay you, I hope."

"Let's not worry now about me getting paid," I said. "Just mail me the papers that were served on your client right away—but read me the name of the case and the Index Number stamped on the Complaint right now, so I can look up the file myself down at the courthouse and start figuring out a way to get the case dismissed. Everything else is secondary."

Everett said, "You seem to know about this stuff. I feel better already."

I headed to the Clerk's Office at the N.Y. County Courthouse next morning armed with the Index Number. A brief conference with the Clerk, who I knew personally from my own litigating adventures and misadventures, led me to realize there were several technical omissions and irregularities in the legal papers, which sought a preliminary injunction against Everett's client, over which I suspected there was no New York jurisdiction. The lawyers whose names were on the papers were from a "white shoe" firm not known for its litigating skills. Back in my office, I immediately started preparing a Motion to Dismiss, or in the alternative, for Denial of the Preliminary Injunction, based on the technical omissions in their papers. While I knew that even if my motions were granted, the papers could be re-done, re-served on Everett's client, and the case started all over again. I knew this would be a major embarrassment to that firm, and what better way to demonstrate to them what they were in for.

I explained my strategy to Everett on the phone so that he could be the one to query the client. He was delighted. I made sure he kept all contact with his client, whom I never met or talked to, so that Everett would have more legal time recorded to be able to bill the company. After I served my Motions and appeared in the Motion Part of the courthouse for argument, I met my young adversary in the Clerk's office while awaiting our turn before the judge. After chatting him up a bit I explained that the defendant company was incorporated in Texas, had no offices or business in the State of New York. So even if he re-filed the case after correcting the technical errors, he would probably never be able to acquire jurisdiction over Everett's client.

"Why not simply withdraw the Motions and drop the case, so that your firm can send it to a firm in Houston, where this company does business and where there can be no doubt about proper jurisdiction?" I inquired.

"Can you wait while I telephone the partner I work for?"

"Sure," I agreed, thinking that by this stratagem, even if they did re-file in Houston, Everett would have more legal business, and I would find a friendly Houston litigator for him to work with.

He came back after the call and told me we had a deal. And so the case was over, and everyone appeared to have gotten some of what they sought. Everett was immensely pleased and said he would not forget this favor. I did not pay much attention to the remark and went back to handling my cases.

Amazingly, when I had completely forgotten about him, some seven months later Everett called again. This time he was ecstatic with the news that the entire Vollbrecht management team had been hired to run a mega-defense contractor named Aerojet General Corporation, located in

El Monte, California, that he was one of its new Senior Vice Presidents and also its General Counsel, and he stated assuredly, "Bob, you are our new outside counsel for *everything*!"

Within several weeks he called to retain my firm to handle Aerojet's acquisition of a New York City plant construction company named Chemical Construction Corporation. It was a very large corporate transaction and I was worried as to whether my firm did indeed have the expertise to staff the various specialties involved in a large acquisition. The name partner who specialized in such matters assured me that his people could do the job. Since this was my client I asked to get copies of all papers and to be kept informed of the progress on the matter, and he assented readily. While I specialized in litigation, I did have a decent grasp of corporate transactions, and in particular, the manner in which the Federal government played a role in approving certain mergers, from my days in the Justice Department. After a month of negotiations and document drafting I was informed that my firm's lawyers were on the way to a closing in two weeks. I thought to ask how the Federal Trade Commission had so quickly given its approval. I was met with a blank stare from the mid-level partner working with several others on the deal.

"Omigosh!" he murmured. "I think we neglected to file with the FTC."

I went quietly ballistic, scrambling to get the firm to do whatever could be done on a crash basis. Of course, it is not so easy to rush a government agency and the closing was delayed several weeks. Everett was rightfully quite annoyed.

"The company will survive the delay; but as their General Counsel, I've been embarrassed, and I have to tell you that I don't think I can allow your firm to handle any more major corporate matters for us. But as to litigation, you can rest assured that you will always be our man. Perhaps you should consider changing firms."

So, I accelerated my efforts to solve the problem I had been musing over for several years.

I went in to see the older of the founding partners, whose clients—Rolls-Royce Engines, Ltd., General Electric Company, and ITT—were then the primary billing clients of the firm, explaining to him that the talent base of the firm was sadly lacking, gave him a quick recital of the Aerojet near disaster, and pointed out that several of our former competitor firms had doubled in both size and capability in the last several years. Despite all of our evenings together, he appeared uninterested. I told him that if the firm was unwilling to strengthen itself by hiring more talent and paying competitive compensation for it, I would be forced to leave since, besides my existing smaller clients, I was now the outside lawyer for Aerojet General and would not be able to develop this client with our present group of lawyers.

He asked, "Where are they located?"

I said, "El Monte, California."

Incredibly, he then said, "Well, you know this firm has never done very well with out-of-state clients."

That was too much for me, and I shot back, "And what about Rolls-Royce Engines of Derby, England. That's not out-of-state, is it?"

I told him quite politely that there was little point to continuing the discussion any further and that I would be, at my own speed, arranging my plans to leave the firm, and I left his office.

Knowing that staying on was foolish, I returned to my unfinished idea of leaving to start my own firm with two young associates, who now worked for me, were very talented and showed signs of developing into extremely successful lawyers. My plan was to spring out in that manner, thus announcing our availability to the galaxy of growing firms that had been pirating talent from sleepy firms like the one I would be leaving.

I almost could not believe the next development. The phone rang in our apartment the following evening. My wife answered and came to me with her hand over the receiver while I was watching the evening news and said:

"It's Bob Young for you."

He was an older partner who had been with the firm for years and had no clients of his own at all. He said to me, "I heard that you're planning to leave with two associates and start your own firm. Is that right?"

I admitted that it was correct.

"Well, Harold and I would like to join you. We think it could be very successful and we don't want to remain in the limited world of Rolls-Royce and GE. So, think it over and try to let us know as quickly as you can."

I agreed to do so. I told my then wife that two minutes was all I needed to think that one over. I immediately rejected the concept of voluntarily placing myself back under older less-talented lawyers because they saw me as an opportunity for them. I waited two days and then very politely told them that I could not agree to taking so many of the firm's talented counsel away at one time. Whether they believed me or not I didn't care.

I did telephone my close friend Tet Sato about my

decision and he was delighted, and I knew he would be a strong supporter of my move. Unfortunately, my wife wasn't. She was terrified of the risk.

"How will you continue to support our two little girls and me?" was the question she was hesitant to finally ask.

I explained, "I have researched my idea quite a bit and have learned from others that if one intends to start a new firm he must have enough money set aside in the bank so that he needs no income for six months, since it takes that long for potential clients to figure out you've moved, to locate your new card or address, to phone you, for you to do some billable work, to bill it, and then to get paid. We have six months covered in the bank, and I'm doing it."

She was never supportive, had little confidence in my skills or me, and was always scared. To be honest, this probably contributed somewhat to our later divorce.

In 1973, we launched the law firm of "Layton and Sherman" at 50 Rockefeller Plaza, which prospered enormously and gave us remarkable freedom, a ton of fun, and the ability to try cases more traditional firms would refuse; to do such cases, where appropriate, for no fee—and occasionally, to do much harm to the malefactors of great wealth.

25

Entry Into the World of International Arbitration

In November of 1975 my legal practice was only marginally involved with the affairs of the Chemical Construction Corporation ("Chemico"), since that New York based company, with its principal offices located at One Penn Plaza, across the street from the Pennsylvania Railroad Station, had its own General Counsel, who appeared quite competent to me. My only task had been to review, at the request of Everett Lowe, all of the plant construction contracts in force at the time of the acquisition of Chemico by Aerojet General.

Those contracts had all been prepared and negotiated by prior Chemico counsel, the firm of Reid & Priest, which I knew and respected. I visited their offices to review and discuss these contracts. Everyone had an arbitration clause providing for resolution of any major disputes pursuant to the Rules of the International Chamber of Commerce, ("ICC") located in Paris, France. In the view of the partners of the Reid & Priest firm, the ICC was the premier international dispute resolution organization equipped to supervise construction disputes of any magnitude, and had an excellent reputation. None of Chemico's plant construction projects had so far resulted in an arbitration dispute. As Chemico's General Counsel had copies of all the contracts, I saw no need to ask for any and concluded my visit.

Remarkably, within days I received an agitated call from Everett, who was then in Paris. All of Chemico, its engineering personnel, executives, translators, and clerical staff, working on its largest project for Sonatrach, the Algerian government's oil and gas agency, had been expelled from the construction site in Arzew, Algeria. Chemico had been served on November 14, 1975 with an ICC Arbitration demand for some $185 million in damages, and the Chemico staff had just arrived in Paris. The top executives were parked at the Plaza Athene hotel, and he directed me to get on a flight to Paris as soon as possible and join him. A room at the same hotel had already been reserved in my name. Before hanging up I did think to ask whether they had been able to get their files on the project out of Algeria with them. The answer was "Not really. Only some basic stuff." The project files were voluminous. I asked for the name of the firm that had filed the arbitration papers and was told that it was Shearman & Sterling of New York City.

One of the first things I did was to secure a copy of the current ICC Rules from the bar association library. I then called Air France for a seat on their next flight, went to my apartment to pack a bag, and headed to JFK for the first of many flights to Paris I would be making over the next several years.

Arriving at the Plaza Athene, I was impressed by its luxurious appointments. I had a very pleasant but modest room. There was a message from Everett that I should join him and some others in the downstairs bar, where they were having drinks before dinner. They were all in quite a rumpled state. The Algerians had managed to scare the hell out of them. They weren't in the frame of mind to discuss plans going forward, but just wanted to tell stories about how they had managed to get from the construction site to Algiers, surrounded by lots of Algerian soldiers, and eventually onto a plane with the baggage they could carry. Everett was accompanied by Elliot Humrich, Chemico's chief translator, John D. Nichols, the executive VP of both Chemico and Aerojet, and Herman Stilgenbauer, Chemico's Chief Engineer. Following dinner, we all agreed to meet in John's suite at 9 a.m. the following morning to plan some strategy.

Nichols' suite was huge and extremely luxurious. I

realized that failed negotiations or not, these guys were going to treat themselves well. One of the first things we discussed was how we were going to staff the case. Everett said that he was going to rely on me as the master of ceremonies for our defense team—that is, to hire the right defense counsel, experts, appoint our arbitrator, etc. The company had used the Paris law firm of Chambaz et Suermont for its normal corporate compliance work, which comprised five French lawyers completely unfamiliar with arbitration. So, we could not make use of them other than in tasks such as closing down the Algerian subsidiary. I suggested that we first concentrate on reading the Sonatrach Claim documents, which spelled out the basis for their seeking such a huge amount in damages, along with the Contract itself. Among the first things that struck us was the standard limitation of liability provision, which in this contract was10% of the contract price of $327,267,000, unless there existed proof of gross negligence.

So there was our first great strategic goal: to prove there was no gross negligence on Chemico's part. In order to demonstrate that Chemico was not guilty of gross negligence, it would be necessary to prove in our filings that Chemico had been doing a professional job until it was fired. Apparently, the high damage claim was brought about by Sonatrach, having replaced Chemico with the Bechtel Corporation on a cost-plus-profit basis. If the case was lost, our client would be paying for Sonatrach's having a plant furnished with gold doorknobs due to the cost-plus-terms insisted on by Bechtel.

As the offices of the ICC were nearby, I made a quick visit to meet the Assistant Counsel in charge of the file. I wanted to learn the procedures that were to take place, as well as to get some suggestions for a well-known arbitrator whom we might appoint on behalf of Chemico. The Assistant Counsel gave me the names of well-known European arbitration specialists, as well as suggested that I might wish to request more time to answer the Arbitration Demand in view of the company's expulsion from Algeria and lack of its files. I thanked him for his help, and then made an appointment to visit an old friend who was now in the Paris office of a firm named Surrey & Morse, that was headquartered in Washington, D.C.

He was extremely helpful, knew a great deal about the ICC and European-style arbitration, but unfortunately had been asked to do some legal work for Sonatrach, for which work was still ongoing. I was disappointed, but he did give me a number of names of prospective arbitrators and strongly suggested that we interview them personally, rather than rely on telephone questioning. The more I asked for the names of candidates, the more I received some names repeatedly, so the task became easier and narrowed down to one or two possibilities. We eventually chose a Mr. John Hudson, an American lawyer living in Paris, who had an excellent reputation, was well-versed in the world of international arbitration, and had the ability to understand the manner in which large U.S. companies function. As he was completely fluent in French, he had the ability to explain our positions clearly to the other two arbitrators.

On returning to New York, I contacted Joseph McLaughlin at Shearman & Sterling, who I found was in charge of Sonatrach's case. I needed to work out a way to get our files back, for without them, we could not defend the case. He informed me that Sonatrach had gotten an order of attachment against Chemico in a local Algiers court, which allowed them to seize Chemico's files; but I pointed out that such a tactic, when properly explained to the Arbitrators, would make it appear that the Algerian firm was using high-handed and unfair tactics to gain advantage over a foreign contractor. McLaughlin understood what I could do with such an argument and it did not take us long to agree on a compromise.

We agreed that they could continue what they were

doing, which was photocopying most of our files, for ten more days, at which time, all of the company's original files would be turned over to my law firm. He also agreed that I could have an extension of our time to answer his Demand (Complaint) in the arbitration, and I agreed that he could have a substantial additional period within which to name Sonatrach's arbitrator. We also had a brief discussion about trying to agree on a Chairman of the panel, which did not get very far.

I had made very little progress in finding a Paris law firm, or a branch of a U.S. firm, that could represent us well in such a large arbitration. At this stage international arbitration was not a field that had attracted large law firm interest. By complete serendipity, I was invited by Mitch Rogovin, a good friend who was in town from D.C., to join him at a dinner party at the home of wealthy friends on Fifth Avenue, who were short a man for their table. I accepted since it was an opportunity to spend some time with him as well as to meet new people. One of the other dinner guests that night was Charles Torem, who was the head of the Coudert Brothers office in Paris. I explained to him that I had just returned from Paris in connection with the Sonatrach arbitration and was looking for a firm qualified to defend such an arbitration. He said that he was familiar with the case, the largest one to have been filed to that date. He was all over me, extolling the virtues of his partners as well as his knowledge of the arbitration world from his position as the U.S. representative on the ICC Council. I inquired whether he would be barred from working on our defense due to his position on the Council. His quick response was that he would be able to work that out due to his excellent contacts at the ICC. He invited me to call him on my next visit to Paris to be his guest for lunch at his club. He took one of my cards, called me at my office the following day in order to further explain the advantages of having my client represented by Coudert Brothers, which had offices in both NYC and Paris, expertise in the handling of cases before the ICC, familiarity with French law, etc. It was hard not to be impressed by his aggressive business-getting abilities and I didn't as yet have a better solution.

I discussed the issue with Everett who said he would leave that decision to me, but that he wanted me and my firm to be heavily involved in the defense, particularly in connection with the written Memorials, which were elaborate briefs with attached exhibits, and an important required step in the procedure of the arbitration. In view of the defense we were going to have to make to the charge of *faute lourde*, or gross negligence, we would have to demonstrate that all of the parts of the plant that Chemico had completed were structurally sound and of a professionally acceptable quality, i.e. we would be rebuilding the plant in our answering papers. As we didn't have enough associates for that task we came up with the concept of "contract lawyers", hired to work on a specific case at a good salary, with no commitment from the firm of being kept on after that case was over, and without benefits, or vacations. Within two weeks, by word of mouth, we had hired two excellent attorneys and were able to slow down our recruiting efforts, although we still kept our eyes alert for additional hires.

By that time the original Chemico site files had been delivered to us by Shearman & Sterling, and the contract lawyers were able to start making use of them with the help of some Chemico engineers. Also, Aerojet management had made the decision to start quietly winding Chemico down. With the loss of the Sonatrach job there were only two other contracts being worked on in the company, not enough business to keep it going for long.

I had to fly back to Paris in order to make some additional hiring decisions. I saw Torem for lunch and retained him and his firm as defense counsel. Reminding him that I was doing this because of being impressed by him, I repeated that I assumed he would be able to represent us in the arbitration. He had brought along a young American partner, Laurence Craig, whom he described as an experienced litigator. They made an early important suggestion that they schedule an appointment to interview Professor Berthold Goldman of the Paris II Law School, as a potential expert on ICC procedures, and quickly pay for his time for the interview, thus preventing Sonatrach from ever hiring him to appear against us. What developed over the following weeks was entirely unexpected.

When I met with Craig, I realized that he was not very experienced as an arbitration litigator or as an expert on Algerian (French) law. When I asked how French law would treat issues that I was certain would arise in the arbitration—such as the poor performance of the Algerian subcontractors that Sonatrach insisted that Chemico hire— he had no better idea than I as to the manner in which French law would reach a decision. The firm probably had other partners learned in French law but I made a decision that I thought could solve two problems. I phoned Professor Goldman and made my own second appointment with him at his home office quite near the Plaza Athene. He seemed pleased to see me again. I told him that I was not satisfied with Coudert's expertise in French law and that I would like him to serve as our French law expert. I would arrange for Coudert to provide Craig's assistant to serve as his research assistant, making use of the Coudert library as well as the library of his law school. He was delighted, and accepted the task with alacrity. Incidentally, his command of English was excellent. I should add that we never had anything but success with our handling of French legal issues.

Our first setback should not have surprised me. Torem phoned me to say the ICC had ruled that he could not participate as counsel in the arbitration due to his position on the ICC Council. So the principal lawyer I wanted on our side from his firm was unavailable, and I felt quite miffed but it was too late to do much about it.

I went about conducting other interviews. In particular, I needed an expert on Swiss law, as the arbitration clause provided that the hearings would be held in Laussane, and much case law indicated that the law applicable in Laussane would control certain procedural issues. I arranged to interview Pierre Lalive in his Geneva law office, along with a client representative, and we had little trouble in deciding that he should be our man. In his mid-sixties, handsome, with a full head of white hair, he was, as was Goldman, fluent in English and extremely qualified in the arbitration field as both a scholar and practitioner. If nothing else, I was pleased with our two legal experts.

Despite several phone and letter exchanges between me and Joe McLaughlin regarding a possible agreement on the Chairman of the arbitration panel, no progress had been made, and the parties had no choice but to leave the selection to the ICC in accordance with its Rules. These provided that the Court of the ICC would chose a member country, whose local ICC Committee would chose one of its panel members to be our Chairman. Not surprisingly, the Swiss committee was chosen. Shortly thereafter, McLaughlin and I were informed via letter that a Maitre Paschoud of Lausanne would be the Chairman of our panel, and thus the deciding vote in the case. All of our efforts to learn about his background brought little information, other than that he was a successful local lawyer about 55 years old with an undistinguished background. His performance during the proceedings was entirely consistent with that sketchy information. In the interim, Sonatrach had named a Professor Maheau of the Algiers Law School as its arbitrator.

The Panel met and soon issued its Terms of Reference for the proceeding, which spelled out a schedule for the filing of Memoires, Counter-Memoires, eventual witness hearings in Geneva, and final arguments (*plaidoirie*) in Lausanne.

Sonatrach's opening Memoire landed on us with a thud. It was over 200 pages in length, with 50 or 60 attached exhibits, and was a formidable production. As it was divided into subject areas, such as Performance of Subcontractors, Adequacy of Cement Supplies, Supervision of Construction Crews, etc., we decided to assign lawyers to those subject areas, making each responsible for preparing a complete response to the many charges leveled against Chemico's performance. I arranged, through Mr. Stilgenbauer, for the assistance of Chemico engineers in developing legal responses to the charges. In addition, we hired our own expert witnesses for critical areas, such as cement; we were fortunate in being able to retain as our overall expert, Mr. Maurice Brooks, the retired former head of Lummus Engineering, who happened to be the father of one of our young partners. He supervised the preparation of the output of our young associates, had a deep understanding of how such a project should have been run, and was able to identify the many ways in which Sonatrach personnel interfered with, or caused the suspension of, portions of the work effort. A clause in the contract, one that had been vigorously resisted by Chemico in its negotiations, provided that *"Wherever possible, preference must be given by Contractor to the use of local Algerian labor."* This proviso alone, we were able to demonstrate, caused enormous delays and difficulties.

In New York, once again, I discovered in conversations with the old management of Chemico, who were kept on for a period by Aerojet, that Chemico had been able to win the award of the contract, by the payment of large commissions to key Algerian players, who would smooth out difficulties as they arose. In this case, there were $15.5 million paid in commissions. The usual procedure was to use the commission agents when the time came to seek supplemental payments for "extras" caused by the demands of the Owner. That is what Chemico, led by Mr. Nichols, should have tried to do here, but in the negotiations over the "extras" requested by Chemico in order to complete the job with a profit, Nichols refused to make use of the commission agents, as he thought the practice was more than likely illegal. According to the old management, that decision doomed the "extras" negotiations and Aerojet deserved the forced evacuation and the arbitration headache. They couldn't believe the *squareness* of the Aerojet "Harvard Business School trained" management.

On my several trips back to Paris, I met with Professor Goldman frequently, especially to review the legal sections of the Sonatrach opening Memoire. Both he and Sonatrach made much out of a letter signed by Mr. Nichols, inadvertently typed and signed on the stationery of Aerojet General, as its Executive Vice President, taking a very aggressive stance over the refusal by Sonatrach to make additional contract payments. I explained that Nichols was prepared to testify, or submit an affidavit, explaining that his secretary had made an error in using Aerojet stationery, for he was sending this letter in his capacity as Executive VP of Chemico! Goldman was adamant in stating that such testimony was impermissible in French law, since, in France, all employees were presumed to be willing to perjure themselves on behalf of an employer. Thus, their testimony was never admitted in French court proceedings. We had no way of convincing the Panel that Aerojet was not attempting to interfere in Chemico's negotiations with Sonatrach. Goldman continued to be troubled by the impact of that letter on the issue of Chemico's alleged "gross negligence". I did not agree with him. However, the letter written on the wrong stationery also had relevance to an effort being made by Sonatrach to bring both Aerojet and the General Tire and Rubber Corporation, the parent of

Aerojet, into the litigation.

That effort at the time was being made at first only by letters sent from Shearman & Sterling to both Aerojet and General Tire, advising of developments in the arbitration and making the claim that the two parent companies would be responsible for payment of any damage award in the arbitration. Even a cursory examination of international arbitral case law in this area revealed that these letters were of no effect legally.

Sonatrach should have named Aerojet and General Tire as Respondents in the arbitration, and then there may have been a justifiable claim of legal responsibility. But now, that error having been made by Shearman & Sterling, we were not going to permit such an obvious end run to be successful.

So the next thing we knew Sonatrach brought suit in the U.S. District Court in New York City against General Tire, Aerojet, and Chemico for alleged antitrust violations, as well as contract breaches. Thus, the two parent companies required attorneys to represent them in that suit. Sound easy? Well, it wasn't.

When I informed the General Counsel of General Tire, Mr. Tress Pittenger, of this development, he had already read the Complaint served on those three companies and said that company policy restricted use of counsel in New York to ten firms, listed in order of preference, and that I must use that list. The list did not surprise me, as it contained only the largest and most prestigious of New York's "white shoe" firms. This development had more than one consequence—it also opened the eyes of major Wall Street firms to the existence of large fee-generating cases that emanated from the arbitration process. I believe it fair to say that many of my later competitors for large arbitration cases were thus alerted to the existence of a field that they had no knowledge of or thought unworthy of their talents.

As to the list, I started with the first name: Sullivan & Cromwell, an easy elimination, as they represented El Paso Natural Gas, which was involved in the LNG plant at issue in the case. At each of the firms, I spoke to the head of their Litigation Group, some of which I knew personally. The second listed firm simply said "No thanks," as did the next seven on the list. Several of the partners that I knew explained that their firm viewed litigation outside their existing corporate clients as unproductive. It also became clear to me that few of them yet understood anything about international litigation and the large fees that it often generated.

I was down to the tenth firm on the list, which was Milbank, Tweed, Hadley & McCoy, and realized if I struck out there, it would be off to Philadelphia, D.C. or perhaps Boston for my co-counsel, and I really did not want the inconvenience of working long distance with an out-of-town firm. A law school classmate named Ed Reilly, happened to be a young partner at Milbank so I phoned him immediately. He was very pleasant, recalling that we had worked together in defending against a weak lawsuit while I had still been at my old firm, but he said he couldn't help me because he had not had a vacation in two years and had promised his son a sailing trip in August. I countered that the first item to take place in this new Sonatrach case was going to be our motion for a stay of the proceeding pending the outcome of the arbitration. There would be at least a month's delay while the Judge decided the motion. By then, he would be back from his well-earned holiday. He said he had to talk it over with his senior partner, but that it might work. The following day he reported that my suggestion was acceptable, and we had new co-counsel in Manhattan.

It developed that Judge Kevin Duffy, who was assigned the antitrust case against General Tire, et al., granted our motion in increments of six months, requiring us to report on progress in the arbitration each time. Thus, we never did have to litigate that case. Meanwhile, on return from vacation, Ed was inundated with his former caseload and we got, as his replacement, his immediate superior, William Jackson, who was the son of Robert H. Jackson, a former Supreme Court Justice, and who was apparently pleased by the prospect of extensive travel to Paris. He also reported on all developments to Mr. Pittenger at General Tire, taking that task off my hands.

Chemico was downsizing its engineering staff rapidly, letting its more recent hires go first, while keeping its employees with seniority on longer. However, a lawsuit was brought against it by one of its more recent hires named Rubin Kremer, who was let go, on the alleged grounds of religious and age discrimination. He had no lawyer and brought it *pro se*. It was completely without merit as Chemico's records did not even list the religion of employees and Kremer was younger than most of the other personnel who were let go, so I assigned the case to a young associate with instructions to do very little work on it as it was no threat to the client.

Despite my instruction, the associate, Donald Crook, told me when I was next in New York, that he had found a Second Circuit case that would permit us to get the Kremer case dismissed via a summary judgment motion. I rejected the idea saying that was too much legal work for such an unimportant matter. We would simply do nothing and then one day, when the Sonatrach case was in a lull, we would ask the judge for a trial date, then try it for a couple of hours, win it on the merits on the basis of the Chemico records, and that would be the end of it. He was not happy with that strategy because he wanted the experience of arguing a summary judgment motion, but dropped the subject on my insistence—for a while.

On my next trip to Paris I learned, among other things, that Sonatrach, upon hearing that I had switched Professor Goldman to be our French law expert, who would be arguing that law to the Panel, had appointed Maitre J.D. Bredin, Goldman's most successful and famous student, as its French law expert. Goldman was delighted at the news. When I told him, he rubbed his hands together with glee, and said that this would be the legal battle of the Century, and that he very much looked forward to it. I recall him saying to me:

"Bob, you have taken ten years off my age by placing me back in a courtroom once again."

I simply replied, "I assume Bredin must know what he's in for."

I do not think we could have got along any better and I

truly enjoyed working with him, even if he constantly ignored my requests that he pay more attention to the facts of the case.

He would reply: "The facts are your province, my dear boy. I will concentrate on the law, which is critical in this case."

I had been having increasing difficulty making hotel reservations once Paris filled up with large fashion house events and business conventions. On several occasions I wound up staying at a second-class hotel in an inconvenient part of town and decided to do something about it. A thought had occurred to me while I accompanied a friend from the Surrey & Morse office on a weekend viewing of several apartments since he and his wife wanted to improve their living arrangements. On that occasion, I met their real estate agent, an impressive lady who spoke English well. Prior to returning to New York that time, I phoned her and asked if she would look for an appropriate small apartment in a good neighborhood for me. I mentioned the Rue du Bac on the left bank, which had been recommended to me by friends. She agreed to keep my request in mind and took down my New York office phone number.

At the time, the dollar was worth ten francs, so many things appeared inexpensive to me. Incredibly, she phoned me within the week following my return to tell me she had just gotten the listing for a two bedroom, kitchen, small dining area, apartment on the fourth floor of a nice building on the Rue du Bac, which I could have for US $150,000, but she said I must move fast as apartments like this did not come on the market too often and the price was reasonable; she asked if I could get a 10% deposit to her immediately. Fortunately, I had a small account at a bank in Geneva, which I had opened when a recession in the USA scared a lot of us into depositing some money abroad. I wired that bank instructions to wire transfer my balance to the real estate agent, and soon learned that it arrived in time for me to secure the apartment, sight unseen. I had it completely repainted. It later permitted me to have both my daughters spend summer vacations there while they took some fun courses at The Sorbonne and dated local French boys working in a vegetable store on the Rue du Bac. For me, and occasionally also my partner Fred, it was a Metro ride to the Coudert offices as well as to the Shearman & Sterling Paris office where we sometimes met.

The Chemico principal Memoire took a great deal out of all of us, but we, and Maury Brooks, were pleased with it when it was filed. Thereafter, we received Sonatrach's Contre-Memoire, which did its best to respond to our first effort, but I thought it failed and that we had gotten an advantage out of the exchange. We then prepared our Contre-Memoire and the written filings were complete. So we then had to start preparing for the witness hearings in Geneva.

We relied on Pierre Lalive's office to get us a number of rooms in an excellent old Geneva hotel with a fine view of the lake, as we had to be able to have witnesses arrive for a day or two, leave after their testimony, and be replaced, and so on. Our permanent staff in addition to myself was Fred, Edgar Pauk, one of our contract employees fluent in French, Herman Stilgenbauer, Maurice Brooks, Laurence Craig, Elliot Humrich, chief translator, and Jake Parker, our cement expert.

McLaughlin and I had agreed to jointly hire a well-known expert court reporter named Jack Finz, who traveled over by himself, met us at the Intercontinental Hotel, where the testimony took place, showed up every morning at exactly 9 a.m. and delivered daily copy to each side and to each arbitrator each evening. Needless to say, this was an expensive exercise, the cost of which we split, but we thought it necessary.

According to the practice in large arbitrations, each witness' direct testimony was introduced through a detailed affidavit plus exhibits, on which he could be cross-examined by opposing counsel, who had to announce that they wished to do so in advance of the hearings. In this manner not every witness had to show up in Geneva if he was not going to be cross-examined.

Fred Sherman had prepared a competition to keep up morale. There is a huge water spout in the center of Lake Geneva and as each witness arrived, especially the engineers, they were asked to write down on a piece of paper their estimate of the height of the water at its highest point. After some discussion, even some of the lawyers were permitted to participate. The entry fee was $10 for the pot, which would go to the winner. Some of the engineers were using slide rules, others just stared and wrote down calculations. As our preparation for the hearings ended we opened up the answer sheets that had been submitted. Some guesses were thousands of meters apart and others were bunched together closely but one stood out, for it was the exact correct height in meters of the spout—and Edgar Pauk, one of our contract lawyers, submitted it.

"How did you do it, Edgar? Not being an engineer but just a lawyer?" he was asked.

"Simple. I just went to one of those news kiosks where they sell souvenir postcards of Geneva, and of course there was one of the Water Spout in the middle of Lake Geneva and I bought it, which listed the height in meters exactly."

"That was unfair!" some exclaimed.

"Nonsense," Edgar replied. "Someone has to be able to use common sense and why not a lawyer?"

So, amidst some grumbling the contest ended, having well served its entertainment purpose.

The large ballroom at the Intercontinental was used for the witness testimony, with each side's lawyers and paralegals arrayed in a line opposing their adversary's similar array, the principal difference being that the Sonatrach side numbered thirteen lawyers, paralegals, secretaries, while our side numbered six in all. The panel of three arbitrators sat with M. Paschoud in the center facing the two lines of opposing parties. A witness chair was placed at an angle close to the table of the panel. The court reporter sat in front of the arbitral panel, and had the task of recording the oath taken and then the testimony of each witness. Each day as a new witness came forward to give his testimony he was asked by the Chairman to raise his right hand and repeat, "I hereby swear that the testimony which I am about to give will be the truth, the whole truth, and nothing but the truth." The response was always to repeat that statement or to state, "Yes, I will" or some other indication of consent. As one or two witnesses did not speak English, a translator was present to aid the process. The Chair would then always say: "Please state your employment."

It was also a rule of the proceedings that each witness was required to submit his/her direct testimony in advance of the hearings in order that opposing counsel might decide if he desired to cross-examine the witness. Many affidavits were submitted that did not attract cross-examination. As to those, the witness was not required to be present at all. For the remainder, the witness would be sworn, he/she would be asked if the affidavit correctly stated the testimony of the declarant, and the opposing counsel would then take over to perform the cross-examination. This procedure permitted the number of testifying witnesses to be cut down considerably, but due to the number of issues raised by the pleadings in our case we were well into the third week of testimony by the time Sonatrach's principal expert was called to the stand, an Italian who had been the Chief Executive of ENI, Italy's largest design/construct firm, for many years prior to his retirement.

We had his affidavit for several weeks and both Maury Brooks and I had studied it with care and I was prepared to do some heavy cross-examination based on the many questions that Brooks had raised in notes to me during our preparations. I had also seen this Italian gentleman sitting in the back of the room with other members of what might be called the audience each day of the proceedings, and would say "Good morning" or *Buon giorno* if we happened to encounter one another in the men's room.

When called to the stand and asked to raise his right hand and respond to the Chairman's oft-repeated question about being willing to state the truth, the whole truth and nothing but the truth, he responded to the surprise of all, especially the Chairman:

"Ah, Mr. Chairman, the truth…" he began with a heavy Italian accent, "Who knows what the truth is?" A gasp was heard from the audience. Paschoud turned livid, and repeated his question but louder and with anger. The witness quietly stated that he would do his best.

The Chairman then said, as he usually did "Please state your employment." The answer came: "Well, I am now retired from ENI but on my properties, I raise many cattle, horses, pigs, and agricultural crops."

"Aha," replied the Chairman, "The Italian definition of work", which provoked some laughter and titters from the audience, after which he told me that I was free to begin my cross-examination, which I did. Brooks and I had prepared some twenty pages of questions on a yellow legal pad, but I didn't get much past the first page where I asked him, very politely, if he could identify his affidavit for me, which he did. I then asked if he had prepared it.

At first, hesitating, he then said, "Yes".

I then countered, "But I did not realize that you were fluent enough in the English language to write this document."

"I explain to the lawyers and they write it," he said.

I pressed, "So you are saying that your lawyers mostly wrote your affidavit? Is that correct?"

By this time, Paschoud had heard enough. He intervened and said "Mr. Layton, I think we understand. There is no reason for you to continue with your questioning of this gentleman."

Thus, ended the testimony of Sonatrach's principal expert—a victim of his lawyers' errors as well as the Chairman's short temper.

I fully did not expect to see the ex-ENI Chairman the following day, but in the men's room, I once again encountered him. I asked how it was that he was still present even though his testimony was concluded. He replied that no one had told him to depart and as he was being paid 3,000 francs per day he saw no reason to depart as yet, especially as he found the proceedings so interesting. And I wished him good luck and we shook hands.

Amusingly, at a small cocktail party provided by the Intercontinental to commemorate the close of the witness hearings, both McLaughlin and I were chatting with Chairman Paschoud and we asked him if he had found the typed transcripts of the day's testimony that were hand-delivered to the hotel room of each arbitrator each evening useful or helpful in any way. He asked if we meant the small package from the Court Reporter. We replied, "Yes. Has it been of help to you?"

"Why no, we never open those packages; we assumed they were ordered by the two law firms for their own use and not for us; so we never even look at them," he replied.

Joe and I were a little shocked, but finally chuckled at the failure of communication, and dropped the subject forever, never describing it to Jack Finz who had labored so diligently at his job.

The final oral arguments were scheduled to take place several weeks later, in Lausanne, as provided in the Contract. The hotel was selected by the Chairman, who lived there. I had returned to New York at the conclusion of the witness hearings. I needed to make another trip to Paris to go over the speeches of both Professors in advance of the final arguments, and Lalive agreed to come to Paris where Goldman and I would meet with him. Each was to prepare an English version of his speech for me to go over, to be delivered to my hotel room the evening prior to our meeting. To my surprise, when I reported on these arrangements to Mr. Pittenger at General Tire, he said that he wanted to attend that meeting and, as he had never flown on the Concorde previously, he directed me to make Concorde reservations for the two of us, which I did. I asked Goldman, via telex, to have an extra copy of both his and Lalive's paper in English sent along to me for Pittenger, so they knew he was coming.

In the Concorde departure lounge, I left Pittenger for a couple of minutes to make a phone call to my office and, while at the phone kiosks, saw that the woman at the next telephone was incredibly pretty and could be a Hollywood star whose name I did not recall. I overheard her saying goodbye to both of her daughters before she left to rejoin her party in the waiting area. On returning to my seat next to Tress Pittenger, I pointed out the woman to him and asked if he knew what Hollywood star she was. He abruptly said "No" and pointed out a typo I had made on the draft of my oral presentation on the facts. "And look at this error on the next page!" was all he spoke about.

When we boarded the Concorde, I was struck once again by how little headroom there was, and felt claustrophobic, but knew that would pass after take-off, from my one prior Concorde flight. It turned out that my Hollywood mystery lady was seated across the aisle from me, alongside what must have been her husband from his handsome appearance, in the first row of the left hand side. I asked Tress again whether he could now remember her name as we were so close to her. "No," he snapped, following with "And look here on page 22, another bad typo."

I finally gave up trying to guess her name and after we had taken off, I leaned forward and, tapping her gently on the shoulder, said:

"Please pardon my intrusion, but could you please tell me your name. I do know that I've seen you in motion pictures, but my mind has gone blank."

"Why that's perfectly all right. Happens often. I'm Natalie Wood and this is my husband, Robert Wagner. Say hello to the gentleman, Bob." Wagner appeared annoyed by the intrusion, but did mutter a "Hello." I thanked her again, and turning back to Pittenger, said "She's Natalie Wood. What do you think of that?" He grumbled, "Look here, another mistake on the next page." And so, it went.

After checking in at The Plaza Athene, and picking up the packages left for us by Professor Goldman, Pittenger and I headed for the small bar/cafe at the hotel which was still open after the main dining room had closed. When we ordered, Tress asked for oysters, while I opted for something much tamer. After gulping down his oysters, Tress called the waiter back and asked for another order of oysters. I could say nothing. Before we went up to our rooms I said that it was important to read the Lalive/Goldman papers overnight, as our meeting with them was at 10 a.m. some twenty minutes away by taxi.

He agreed and we were to meet for breakfast at 8:30 a.m. I was up for several hours reading the Goldman/Lalive papers, and had few comments or questions. On meeting Tress at the breakfast table, I knew trouble lay ahead. He looked ghastly, face pale, eyes bloodshot from obvious lack of sleep.

"Got terribly sick last night. Must have been a bad oyster. Hardly slept. Kept throwing up. So it's up to you to comment on those papers, which I hardly got to read."

"OK," I said. "I've read them and think they are basically good; so don't worry; leave it to me." He appeared to agree; ate nothing for breakfast, and off we went to the meeting, which was in an office on the third floor of a building with a spiral staircase, but we took the elevator.

This was Pittenger's first meeting with our two foreign law experts, and at the outset it went well. I gave a synopsis of our factual positions, with which they all seemed familiar. Then Goldman explained in summary his view of the effects of French law on those facts, and how he was going to present the French law. So far, so good. Pittenger hadn't said a word other than hello, nice to meet you, etc. Then came Lalive, who explained how Swiss law applied in terms of enforcement of any award, attacking the award, etc. and, seemingly from outer space, I heard Pittenger start talking, criticizing both of their papers—this from the same fellow who told me he hadn't read them and who had agreed that I would handle all the talking in light of his being sick. I recall most clearly from what could only be termed a diatribe, was him telling Lalive something like:

"Where I come from in Akron, Ohio, you first tell your audience what the problem is, then you explain your solution to it, and them remind them again how you plan to solve it."

A long silence and then slowly and quite loud, Lalive said, in so many words:

"Meester Peetinger. Perhaps before zis case is over, you weel understand that it weel be decided under the law of the Republic of Fraunce and not the law of Akron, Ohio!"

Silence from all participants followed. We then packed up our briefcases and with pretended politeness took leave of each other. I told the experts that I would be in touch.

Pittenger decided to walk down rather than wait for the elevator. He asked me as we walked down, I somewhat staggering after him, how I liked the way he straightened out Professor Lalive. I said yes, I heard you, but you know what he responded about French law controlling is undoubtedly correct under the contract.

"Oh, yes?" Pittenger asked. "I had turned off my hearing aid by then and didn't hear a word he said."

I just shook my head and kept walking, hoping I could forget this entire trip.

The locale of the final oral arguments was another large hotel, this time in Lausanne, where both sides of lawyers and paralegals stayed, no witnesses being required. The practice in France was that each lawyer who addressed the Tribunal would at the conclusion of his remarks hand up his notes, typed or handwritten, to the Chairman, which apparently sufficed as a record for the Panel. McLaughlin spoke first, did not do a bad job, and after a short coffee-break intermission, my turn came. I thought it went well.

Incidentally, there were no questions at all put to the counsel by the Panel. Then, Goldman spoke for quite some time in French, quoting extensively from French statutes in his large notepapers. A lunch break was taken, and as I was standing in the rear of the room I spotted Jean-Denis Bredin racing out of the room. I stopped him to say hello and tell him how much I admired some of his better-known legal victories. He interrupted me to say:

"Please pardon me, Mr. Layton, but I must hurry to my room to attempt to prepare some responses to the damage which my mentor and friend Berthold has done to my arguments," and off he dashed.

The following day most everybody departed in different directions, but McLaughlin and I were invited by the Chairman to attend a site seeing tour of Laussane, which he and his wife had arranged for all who cared to climb on the bus. I could not risk leaving McLaughlin alone with the Chair for the day on the bus and had to join the tour. I snatched Edgar Pauk to join me due to his excellent French and European charm; so I sicked Edgar onto Paschoud while I sat next to his wife, who spoke English well. By late afternoon, we had seen it all from the bus, but did enjoy a visit to the home of Oona Chaplain, where the famous actor had once resided. Thence, back to the States where we awaited the issuance of the final Award by the arbitrators.

26

KREMER v. CHEMICO in the Supreme Court

During one of my many trips back to New York our associate who was defending the *Kremer* case had pointed out a new decision by the Second Circuit Court of Appeals, which made it crystal clear, that our motion for summary judgment was a winner. But I had little more time to look into the area and more from weariness than anything else, had told him to go and make the motion. While awaiting the issuance of the final award in the Sonatrach case, our associate was called to court to hear the decision of the District Judge, one Abraham Sofaer, on his motion. He explained to me what had taken place.

Judge Sofaer had handed out copies of his opinion, two pages in length, granting our motion for summary judgment based on the clear precedents of the Second Circuit. But he then said that he disagreed strongly with those precedents and had written a lengthy (27 page) explanation of why they were wrong, citing cases from two other Federal Circuits, which would have ruled against our motion. He had his clerk pass out copies of that explanation which would be attached to his short two-page decision, and he predicted that if an appeal were taken from his decision to the U.S. Supreme Court, it would be successful. Since Mr. Kremer did not have a lawyer but appeared representing himself, the Judge announced that he was going to make sure some capable lawyers would represent Kremer, should he wish to file an appeal! The result could not have been more disastrous. We won a temporary victory but were headed, for the client, toward a mighty expensive road to get rid of what was in reality a nuisance case. In a sense this was my fault for not having continued my insistence that no motion be made, but neither I, nor our associate, could have predicted the bizarre conduct of Judge Sofaer.

The following day I received a phone call from Frederick Schwartz, a partner at the Cravath law firm telling me that he had received a call from Judge Sofaer asking his firm to take on the appeal on a pro bono basis; so we were now opposed by a large firm committed to the case in order to please a sitting district judge.

The Cravath firm filed an appeal to the Second Circuit, which was quickly denied. It then applied for a writ of certiorari to the U.S. Supreme Court, and had succeeded in getting the Solicitor General's Office to join in that application, an apparently brilliant stroke of lawyering. I was impressed by their performance in getting the SG's office on their side, but from my experience in the Justice

Department for three years I was aware that the Solicitor General did not win all of his cases, and was curious as to why the decision to enter my case had been made. Not surprisingly, the writ of certiorari was granted, and so I was going to be presenting my first argument before the Supreme Court in a case that I had properly initially analyzed as being worth about two hours of trial time and could have resulted in a quick and final victory, but where overwork on the Sonatrach arbitration had brought about a careless approval of an associate's ideas, and perhaps a disaster for my client!

The Sonatrach Award, when it was released, provided for a small recovery to Sonatrach, but essentially was a substantial victory for us, as the arbitrators found that Chemico was not guilty of gross negligence, and therefore the 10% of the contract price limitation applied. We were assessed with costs of the arbitration, divided between the parties, and other sundries, reaching a total of $40,000. General Tire authorized me to settle for up to $25,000, which McLaughlin angrily rejected, and so the dance continued on, to my delight.

Meanwhile, the *Kremer* case was scheduled for argument before the Supreme Court in December of 1981 some months after the retirement of Justice Potter Stewart, and the appointment of Sandra Day O'Connor in his place. Fritz Schwartz had been appointed Corporation Counsel of New York City, and his principal assistant on the case was to replace him at the oral argument, joining an Assistant Solicitor General, arguing for the government. Each side is allocated 30 minutes for argument, and I was informed that Cravath had ceded 15 minutes of their time to the SG's office, leaving them with only 15 minutes and me with a full half hour.

I should make it clear that, due to my heavy involvement with travel to Europe and back, and preparation for the Sonatrach final arguments, I had precious little to do with the writing of our brief in the *Kremer* case, other than to read drafts on my airline flights. The brief itself was the work of Dan Brooks, at the time a young partner in the firm, who had a remarkable talent for brief writing. I had asked him on several occasions to file the papers for his admission to the Bar of the Supreme Court, for otherwise a lawyer's name could not appear on an opinion of the Court. Despite my nagging, he never got around to doing it and thus, his name was not listed along with mine and two others from our firm, neither of whom had much to do with the writing of our brief. I used the "Brooks Brief" as my study guide for the argument.

I had given serious thought to bringing my two young daughters, twelve and ten, to Washington for the argument, but decided against it, thinking that there would more than likely be another case before my career was over, and they would be older and able to understand more. As it turned out, I didn't have any more cases in the Supreme Court.

I was up half the night before the argument, re-reading the cases that Brooks had cited, along with large chunks of his brief, and concluded as I had many times in the past, that some of his language just sang with clarity and power. I also recalled with fond pleasure the practice trial at the Barristers Union when I was forced to pinch-hit for my frozen classmate, an event that taught me I could speak to an audience while standing on my feet.

At the oral argument the young Cravath associate told me that he was also permitting the Assistant SG to speak before him. That fellow, whose name shall here be omitted, was incredibly arrogant and taken with his own belief in his brilliance.

When asked by Justice Byron White what the position of the Government was on U.S. Code Section 1283, he responded: "It is the view of the Government that it is not in the case."

White was more than puzzled, as half of the briefs were

devoted to analysis of that Section's import. He queried: "You say that it is not in this case?"

"Yes, Your Honor", came the reply.

"I see", said White as he turned his chair sideways and never asked the fellow another question.

I realized that I now had at least one vote against Mr. Kremer. Justice Thurgood Marshall threw soft balls to the Assistant SG, as did Justice Stevens. Justice Rehnquist launched questions at both counsel arguing for a reversal. Finally, my turn arrived. I was instantly met by hostile queries from Justices Marshall and Stevens, which confirmed the opinion formed during my years in the Office of Legal Counsel when many of us spent our Monday lunch hours listening to oral arguments in this very Courtroom. In those instances, questions never seemed to be asked to get information from the responder, but were just used to make clear how little the Justice asking the question thought of the position of the responder. The counselors were just used as foils by the judges whose sympathies lay elsewhere.

Only when Sandra O'Conner addressed me did I experience being questioned by someone who actually was interested in knowing what I thought and why. She did not have any axe to grind. She was new and was just looking for some answers. It was apparent to me that she had read the briefs of both sides carefully and had made notes of the questions she had and desired to receive some enlightenment if possible. I had the best time explaining our views of the statutes and what had happened in this case and why Mr. Kremer had exhausted his rights in the New York state courts prior to starting all over again in the Federal courts. She very courteously thanked me for my answers, and my time was up and I sat down. I wasn't sure but I thought that I might have one more vote to accompany Justice White's.

As we emerged from the courtroom with all our documents and briefcases, I was stopped by a middle-aged, well-dressed woman, who said to me:

"Please excuse my forwardness but don't you have a weekend home in Lakeville? I believe I have seen you there on Interlaken Road."

"Yes, I do, but I'm afraid I cannot stop to chat right now. My colleagues and I have a plane we must catch."

"Of course, I understand; but I very much enjoyed listening to your argument."

We quickly parted and off we went to the airport.

She, of course, could not restrain herself and wrote a Letter to the Editor of the Lakeville Journal about seeing a

Lakeville weekender arguing a case in the Supreme Court.

Then came a young reporter who wanted to interview me for an article in that paper. When I explained that speaking publicly about the case while it was still undecided by the Court would be a terrible affront to the justices; he said that he could get his Editor to agree not to print the interview until after the decision came down. I was reluctant even to agree to that, but after repeated phone calls each weekend I was there, I finally relented after having drafted a document formalizing the paper's promise not to print until I informed them that the decision had been rendered, and that document had been signed and returned to me. I then gave the interview. I should not have been surprised that the following week, a front-page article appeared about the interview, quoting me extensively; so much for trusting a newspaper.

I was nervous as a cat that some Cravath associate with a weekend house nearby would spot the interview article and get word back to one of the Justices about the newspaper article, thus irritating the Court and causing loss of the appeal. Finally, at the end of May, I was relieved and delighted to get the Opinion and Decision of the Court in our favor by a 5-to-4 vote, with an excellent opinion written for the majority by Justice White, who quoted extensively from the brief written by Brooks. Great satisfaction all around, though not many people understood how it came about that the case wound up in the Supreme Court to begin with.

Years later, I was pleased when my older daughter, Elisabeth, who was then in her first year at the Yale Law School, phoned me to say that she was surprised and delighted to find my *Kremer* case highlighted in her Federal Procedure casebook, where she was able to read my name as the winning Counsel.

It took several more years of wasteful litigation effort on the part of Shearman & Sterling in the U.S. District Court in San Diego, California until a settlement was finally reached between the two sides. Due to Chemico's weak financial condition, and the inability of Sonatrach to get a Court to hold Aerojet or General Tire, the parent or grandparent companies, liable for payment of the Award, we were able to settle this long fought battle for a mere $25,000! I was happy it was finally concluded, and we had to spend a number of hours just deciding which files could be destroyed and which were to be sent to the warehouse.

The good news was the reputation created for me as an expert on the handling of large infrastructure arbitrations in third-world countries. I was asked by MEAD, a company specializing in running conferences on all aspects of Middle Eastern Arbitration issues, to speak at one of its largest conferences in London. There, I was approached by an officer of a U.S. engineering company that wished to retain me to defend the North Yemen Water & Sewerage Company in an ICC arbitration brought against it by a Dutch/British conglomerate. I indicated that my firm would be interested if our expenses to make an investigative trip to Sana in North Yemen would be advanced by the government of North Yemen. As the project at issue in the arbitration was being financed by the U.S. Agency for International Development, U.S. lawyers had an inside track.

We received the $25,000 advance we had requested and Fred Sherman and I flew to Sana and threw ourselves into a fascinating project dispute. We had to return several times to gather facts and documents. Months later a first hearing was held in Paris at the offices of the ICC before a distinguished panel of arbitrators. Fred and I split the arguments between us and, in fairness, we ran circles around the Dutch/English opposition. The proof of that fact came at the end of the hearing when we took our clients, along with their Yemeni local lawyer, Sahid Shobi, to a celebratory lunch at Fouquet's Restaurant on the Champs-

Élysées. When our drinks arrived, Sahid proposed a toast to me for having done such a marvelous job of arguing.

I responded by saying, "That's very nice of you to say, Sahid. But, with respect, how would you know as you are not familiar with the issues I argued."

He responded, "Ah, but I know that during the coffee break the chief executive of our adversary doubled his bribe offer to me from what it was several months ago. That's the best proof to me."

So, it was not a shock to us to discover some months later that the case had been settled quietly without our having been even consulted any further.

I was also asked to write a column on international arbitration for an engineering journal called "International Projects" that I enjoyed doing. On returning to New York from one of the last of my European jaunts, I was pleased to learn that I had been named to the U.S. Committee of the ICC for a five year term, so that it was possible that I might be named to be Chairman of an arbitration where the parties could not agree among themselves on a chair, in much the same way that we had gotten M. Paschoud in the Chemico case. Indeed, I was named Chair in an interesting dispute venued in Puerto Rico, largely I believe due to my knowledge of Spanish.

By this time it was clear that the hitherto, unknown advantages of the international arbitration world in terms of fees, interesting work, and travel overseas, was over. Competition opened up on almost every street corner. Most of the downtown firms at the time threw their hat in the ring, opening up offices in Paris and London, or merging with smaller foreign firms. We had no Paris or London office and were paying the price for it in the loss of business opportunities. So, we explored the opportunities, of which there were many in the traditional New York firms that were looking to expand by way of merger; we were approached by many of them, often through headhunting firms. Alas, none that did international work appeared. I turned to my friends at Surrey & Morse in Paris and found them most interested. In fairly short order, the merger was negotiated and in 1984 we became part of a firm that had offices in London, Paris, Washington, D.C., and New York.

27

The Dragon Lady

While at Layton and Sherman, managing the *Sonatrach v. Chemico* arbitration, and getting to know most of the important players in the company of my new, large client, the Aerojet General Corporation, I received a call from Everett Lowe, its General Counsel, to the effect that an American Arbitration Association case had been filed against Aerojet by its partner in the construction of a munitions plant in the state of Israel. He wanted me to handle the case personally as he knew I had substantial arbitration experience in AAA commercial cases and since he had represented the company in the negotiations that led to the munitions plant contract and wanted to participate in the defense himself.

Our adversary, a Ms. Edith Reich, claimed to be a Holocaust survivor and together with her husband, had recently come to live in Israel, which welcomed them under the Law of Return. She was now running a company that had contracted with Aerojet to build a munitions plant in Israel as part of a joint venture. Munitions were a central part of Aerojet's business as a U.S. defense department contractor.

The arbitration hearing began shortly thereafter at the New York offices of the AAA before three lawyer/arbitrators whom I was somewhat acquainted with. Mrs. Reich had as her counsel the well-known New York firm of Rogers & Wells. Following her counsel's short opening, she took the stand and testified for the first five full days. Most of her claims were entirely new to us, never having heard about any of them in any correspondence between the parties. There was also no documentary support introduced into evidence or any explanation as to why no construction of the plant had begun as yet; nor were any other witnesses presented in support of her story. I knew that the arbitration panel had not expected such a lengthy presentation by just one side and thought they would be amenable to an adjournment in order to spend some time back at their offices; so during a lunch break I asked Everrett for permission to request a 10-day adjournment.

"Why so long?" he asked.

I replied, "Because we have had no time to look into this $40 million claim, and I think the best way to do it is for you to send me to Tel Aviv to attempt to verify some of these claims."

"But that will be very expensive." he replied.

"So is $40 million dollars. In arbitration, you rarely get any discovery of the other side's documents; in this case we are completely in the dark about this woman, her company and whether any of her sworn testimony is true. I think it critical that my trip be authorized. I will fly tourist class if that will help."

Everett said, "First, see if you can get the adjournment. Meanwhile, I will speak to the company president about your trip. But flying tourist is not going to be your best argument."

The Roger & Wells partner objected vehemently to the 10-day adjournment, but to no avail. The business pressures on the individual panel members aided me in getting the requested adjournment. The next morning Everett, along with the Aerojet president phoned me, and after asking some more questions, did authorize my trip flying Business Class and leaving as soon as El Al could find me a seat.

Upon my arrival, I made arrangements to stay at a hotel in Tel Aviv and made telephone appointments to meet with Israeli government officials in charge of munitions and related matters. They were very accommodating and agreed to see me almost immediately when I explained that my inquiry related to a claim for $40 million in damages by an Israeli corporation against a U.S. defense contractor.

Each of the Israeli officials I interviewed in their offices were very polite, tried to be helpful, but were extremely circumspect about not speaking ill of Mrs. Reich. They verified that she and her husband had only immigrated to Israel within the past year and said that they did not know a great deal about them. When I inquired about the approvals that must have been requested for construction of a munitions plant—which I assumed would require some type of defense department approval—they were strangely silent. I was told by more than one official that I should contact a Colonel Yuri Goren, recently retired from the Israeli military forces, who it was said had accepted employment by Mrs. Reich's company. They were able to give me his address and phone number. Incidentally, I was much impressed by the bare-bones offices and simplicity of the trappings surrounding these rather high-ranking officials, together with their work dress, which was short-sleeved khaki shirts, shorts and sandals. That afternoon I phoned Colonel Goren, was pleased to find him in, and invited him to be my guest for breakfast at my hotel the following morning, which he readily accepted. Later in the afternoon I visited the neighborhood in Tel Aviv where Mrs. Reich and her husband lived. On finding their building I located their landlord, confident that they were still in

Manhattan, preparing for cross-examination and the rest of the case.

When I asked the landlord if he knew anything about the case the Reichs had brought against Aerojet General about a munitions plant, his face beamed as he said that he actually owned twenty percent of the Reich's expected recovery, which was an arrangement that had been made in lieu of the apartment rental which they said they could not pay due to the high cost of running the arbitration. He told me he was looking forward to receiving at least a million dollar share in the near future as he was told that Aerojet was a very large and wealthy company and would be likely to settle this case.

I next visited their greengrocer, who told me a remarkably similar tale, the only difference being that his ownership interest was only at fifteen percent. The butcher, tailor, and local laundry stories were identical except for the percentages. I was also introduced to several alleged employees of the Reichs, who also were being paid in part by contingency interests. Before I quit for the day, the total of the interests encountered had exceeded two hundred percent. So I was eager to meet with Colonel Goren the following morning.

Rarely had I met an individual who impressed me as

favorably as had Yuri Goren when we breakfasted together in the courtyard of my hotel the following morning. He was about 45 years old, quite good-looking, still dressed in his military uniform. I had learned from doing a little research and making some inquiries that he was a hero of the Six Day War and very highly regarded in his country. He explained that he put in his retirement papers in preparation for entry into the private world of business in order to improve the financial circumstances of his family, as his entire career had been in the Israeli Army. He had been approached aggressively by Mrs. Reich to join her company in its venture with Aerojet with promises of a large salary, but to date, he had been paid nothing; and from what he had seen thus far, he was convinced that she was a dishonest speculator who was interested in making use of his military reputation. He was not pleased.

We got along extremely well, to the point where I felt comfortable enough to ask if he would be willing to come to New York the following week to attend the remaining arbitration, and possibly give testimony on behalf of Aerojet. I explained that, of course, the company would pay the fare for himself and his wife and put them up in a first class hotel in New York City. He asked to think about it, but in any event could not accept any payments on his behalf by Aerojet, as he would come solely because of his belief that people like Mrs. Reich gave Israel a bad name in the business world, and he wanted to make certain that she was not successful at what he now believed was an effort to embarrass Aerojet into making a large settlement in her favor. I had not met many men of the caliber of Yuri Goren, and was not surprised when he later informed me that his wife agreed with him and they would be coming to New York to assist in any way that they could.

Before leaving Tel Aviv, I managed to contact a reputable litigation lawyer to assist me in getting sworn affidavits from each of the owners of percentage interests in the outcome of the case against Aerojet. At the suggestion of Yuri Goren, I learned that not one step in obtaining permits had been taken by the Reichs, even if the Israeli government would've permitted such a move.

In New York, the arbitration resumed with my cross examination of what had been, until then, a fiercely aggressive presentation by Edith Reich. I asked Yuri to remain outside of the hearing room, in one of the empty offices of the AAA. I then began questioning her, somewhat gently and politely, regarding, amongst other things, her recruiting of Colonel Goren as an executive of her company. I asked whether she had other investors in her company who would profit from any settlement or award against AeroJet. She huffily rejected any such suggestion. By the next morning, the package of properly notarized affidavits had arrived from my local Tel Aviv counsel and I was able to introduce them into evidence.

Mrs. Reich broke into tears, claiming that this was some conspiracy by a large American munitions manufacturer to humiliate and destroy her, that there was no truth to any of the affidavits. At her company's expense, she threatened to bring Colonel Goren to testify so that the panel could learn the truth. I calmly told her that there was no reason for her to go to all that trouble, as I had Colonel Goren outside as my first witness and I asked my assistant to leave the room in order to escort Colonel Goren into the hearing room. The look on Mrs. Reich's face, on seeing the military hero, was priceless, and I knew the case was over.

The panel excused Mrs. Reich from further testimony. They were extremely interested to hear what Colonel Goren had to say, accepted an affidavit that he had prepared together with my local counsel, and said that they were ready to make their ruling. As it was then late on a Friday afternoon, they arranged to transmit copies of their decision by messenger to the office of each counsel by early evening. Everett was convinced Mrs. Reich might still try to bribe the three arbitrators. He had christened her "The Dragon Lady" early in the proceedings and now insisted that my young associate stand watch outside the offices of the arbitration chairman, and that two of his AeroJet employees stand similar watch outside the offices of the other two panel members. He also described in detail to the watchers the appearances of Mrs. Reich's daughter and son-in-law, who were accompanying her and whom he suspected might be used by her as messengers for the bribery attempt. As it turned out, no bribery was attempted to my knowledge.

By 8 p.m., messenger delivery was made to my office and to the office of my opponent—of a short, pungent award, denying all of Mr. and Mrs. Reich's claims against AeroJet and assessing the costs of the arbitration against her and her company.

An arbitration award is a private document. Unless one of the parties challenges it for legal reasons in a court of law, and then the decision of the court does become public and might draw some newspaper attention. I was sorry about that, because I was of the view that the Reichs were not retiring from the field of fraud and would be heard from again. When I mentioned my regret that we had done nothing to alert the business world to the Reichs' scandalous tactics, Everett laughed out loud and said that his bosses would crucify him if he spent company money to warn other businesses about the "Dragon Lady".

"Nice job. Let's forget about her now."

It shouldn't be surprising that one day, several years later, I read a front-page article in *The Wall Street Journal* about how a female Israeli con artist had defrauded a large, Dayton, Ohio corporation out of millions of dollars. The company, named Dayco, had sued her and her husband and recovered a judgment for millions of dollars, but had been unable to collect a penny of it as the Reichs claimed successfully, that they were judgment proof. I clipped the article and mailed a copy to Everett but he never did reply. I kept up a correspondence with Yuri Goren for several years and met him again when he was visiting New York.

In May of 2006, it came to my attention that Mrs. Reich and her married daughter, Bridgette Jossem, lost another case in the Federal courts and had a judgment in the amount of $200 million dollars entered against them. Thus, it can be seen that there was nothing small-scale about The Dragon Lady.

28

The Imperial Government of Ethiopia v. Baruch Foster Corporation

Prior to my involvement in the Sonatrach/Chemico arbitration, I had been a follower of the efforts in the United Nations to codify the manner in which awards entered in international arbitral disputes could be enforced. I had studied those efforts while at the Office of Legal Counsel at Justice, and knew that the Treaty providing for enforcement of Awards had recently come into force but no case had yet been filed under its aegis. One of the lawyers sharing our offices at 50 Rockefeller Plaza, Charles J. Lipton, was a classmate of mine who did a great deal of work for African states that could not afford regular legal fees. The fees that he charged, to his great credit, were quite low.

He spoke to me one day about an arbitration case where he had been helping the Ethiopian Government and its Swiss trial lawyer, who turned out to be the brother and law partner of Pierre Lalive, who I later hired as our Swiss counsel in Sonatrach. The Ethiopians won the arbitration but did not have contacts in the U.S. who knew how to enforce their Award against a Texas corporation named Baruch Foster. I told him that I knew exactly how to enforce such an Award and would be delighted to handle the matter but could not do it on a pro bono basis. We communicated via telex and worked out a satisfactory fee arrangement. I then drafted the Motion to confirm the Award, which was all that was required under the "New York Convention", had them send us a notarized and official copy of the Award from the ICC; then we all re-read the draft Motion and when it was approved, I located an excellent local counsel in Dallas, who was instructed to serve and file the Motion as soon as possible.

Charles Lipton and I flew down to Dallas to attend the hearing on our motion to enforce the arbitral award against Baruch Foster that came on before an extremely able Federal District Judge. I was heard first in support of the motion to confirm the Award and spent little time disposing of the lame argument that the Chair of the panel, Professor Renee David, had a disqualifying conflict of interest because since, years earlier he had been asked by the Government to draft the Ethiopian civil code. As this was a matter of national knowledge, equally well known to Baruch Foster, which made no objection to his selection as Chair, it hardly deserved much consideration as a reason not to enforce the Award. We had also filed an Affidavit by Professor David affirming that his prior drafting of the Code had no impact on his service as arbitrator.

The District Judge was polite but firm in rejecting the argument put forward by the Baruch Foster counsel, and entered an Order confirming the Award. As we left the courthouse I spoke to my adversary, suggesting that if his client paid the full amount of the Award straightaway, I would recommend to our client that a discount off the full amount be considered. He said that they would consider my proposal. Several days later they notified our local counsel that no payment would be forthcoming, thus bringing about an appeal by Baruch Foster to the Fifth Circuit Court, then sitting in St. Louis. I was not unhappy with the result, since I was positive the Fifth Circuit would affirm and preferred having a higher court decision on this case of first impression under the UN Convention.

I did not trouble Charles Lipton to join me on the trip to St. Louis for the hearing as I was confident of the result. The argument before the higher court was indeed brief and resulted in an *affirmance* in fairly strong words. This time, Baruch Foster had no choice other than to pay, as interest charges were continuing to run. The entire experience was greatly pleasing to me as it enabled me to secure the first enforcement of an arbitral award under the UN Convention under circumstances where the arbitration bar in Europe, as well as the United States, undoubtedly followed the case. The Ethiopian government was pleased as were we all.

29

Losing a Good Friend

Every December, I would usually bump into Al Lowenstein, my law school classmate, in the men's locker room of the Yale Club, after a game of squash. Al often worked out in the gym, having been a college wrestler. He would usually say to me, "Layton, what are you up to these days?"

I would always answer, "Litigating, Al; same as always." That would be our contact for the year unless I did receive an invitation to his annual Christmas party in the mail and decided to locate it out in the wilds of Brooklyn. Usually, however, the invitation would arrive several days after the party had been held. That year, 1978, was different. Al actually started a conversation with me by asking, "Where is your office?"

"In Rockefeller Plaza, where it's been for the last five years," I replied.

Al asked, "Do you have any extra offices?"

"Why?" I countered.

"Well, the place where I am now, Delson & Delson, near the UN buildings, is unhappy with me because I haven't brought in enough business for them to cover my rent bill so they're throwing me out."

"I find it hard to believe you haven't brought in much business. You know every pol there is. You've been a congressman. I ought to know. I've contributed to every one of your campaigns, most of them unsuccessful, recently."

"Now don't rub it in, Bob; I came very close last time."

"Forget about that, Al. If you're really in need of an office, we can help you out since we often rent offices to single practitioners, but for you there would be no cost since you've done so many things that my partners and I strongly support. So, let's have lunch here, say, Thursday at 1 p.m. in the Tap Room. I'm going to bring my partner Fred Sherman along. Now, don't stand us up, which I recall, you've sometimes done in the past."

"Don't worry about that," said Al. "I'll be there with bells on."

So, when back in our offices at 50 Rockefeller Plaza, I explained my chat with Al to Fred, who was wildly enthused. "I've always admired what he's done, Bob. I think it would be highly popular with the rest of the staff— and we certainly don't need the rent income from Al."

The three of us then had lunch as planned—and Al showed up on time. We worked out some of the details of the arrangement. When I asked if he had a secretary, Al replied, "Well, I have a young lady volunteer from my last campaign who handles my phone calls, which are many, and types an occasional letter, but no legal stuff."

"Okay, you can bring her, but we won't be paying her any salary," I said.

Al agreed, and they both showed up the next day with their files and extensive Rolodexes. Al was in the telephone business; I never saw his phone not busy. He was an excellent politician, never failing to say "good morning" to every one of our secretaries, ask about their families, or compliment them on an especially pretty dress. He was great for the morale of the office. I noticed that there did not appear to be any income-producing work; it was all pro-bono or Democratic politics. Governors or Senators were always calling.

"Al, you have great contacts. Use them to bring in a civil lawsuit or two…or three. We will do them for you—for no fee. You will get the fees and then you can start to save some money," I advised.

He had told me that he had no savings accounts or stocks and would do as I suggested, but he never did, and I'm not sure he even tried.

One morning, late in October, he came into my office to

ask for a 'favor'. I said, "Sure, name it."

He explained that Ted Kennedy's presidential campaign wanted him to go to the Miami Beach area in Florida to campaign and fund raise for Kennedy's primary race but they couldn't give him expense money at this time and said he would be compensated well at a later time. So, he asked if the firm could lend him $1,000 for expenses for his trip. I hesitantly said, "No, we won't do that."

Al looked at me somewhat puzzled.

I continued, "But we *will* lend you $5000. I can't let you go around like a pauper. I'll sign a firm check and you can take it downstairs to our bank on the first floor and get the cash. Pay it back when convenient. Do you have a place to stay down there?"

"Yes," he replied. "I own a condo in Miami Beach, my only asset, so that's not a problem."

I asked him to call if he needed any other help and wished him well. His secretary stayed with us and kept him informed about all his phone messages. I didn't hear from him until March of 1980 when he called to tell me his Kennedy campaign tasks were finished and he was coming back to New York, arriving the next day and wanted to meet for lunch at the Yale Club so that he could pay back the money we had lent him. Of course I agreed, telling him that I looked forward to seeing him. The date was March 14, 1980. At lunch, he told me how successful he was getting the older Jewish voters lined up to support Ted Kennedy. The Kennedy people knew he was very popular with those Miami Beach area voters and seemed pleased with his performance at both vote getting as well as fund raising and he told me that they had paid him well and now he wanted to pay us back. He pulled a huge role of $100 bills out of one of his pants pockets and started counting them off.

"Did they pay you in cash?" I asked.

He said, "Yes."

I expressed surprise, thinking that might violate some federal campaign regulations, but let it drop. When he got to having counted out $4,000, I told him to stop.

"Why don't you hold onto the rest to make sure you have some walking-around money and you can pay us the rest a little later."

So, I knew he had at least $1000 on him. We walked back to our offices up Fifth Avenue, and I asked him what his schedule was like for the afternoon.

"Besides returning a large number of phone calls, I have one of my former students from Stanford coming in to see me. His name is Dennis Sweeney and I haven't seen or heard from him in several years, and I'm a little curious as to what's on his mind."

"By the way," I said, "we have to let the telephone company do some work this afternoon in the office that you were using, so we had your secretary move your desk stuff into the larger office, catty corner from mine. I hope you don't mind."

"Of course not. Larger is better," he said.

We each went to our offices. I had some long distance calls to make so I closed my office door and when I came out once to speak to my secretary, I noticed that Al's door was closed as well.

Around 4 p.m. that afternoon, I heard a strange noise from the nearby office that Al was using and the staccato, abrupt cracks sounded like noises that might be made by the phone repairman. I went out of my office to inquire and was horrified to see a tall, thin man standing in Al's doorway, holding a pistol in his hand, and Al, lying crumpled on the floor beside his desk.

I pulled myself together sufficiently to ask this visitor if he would please put the pistol down on the desk next to a sofa in our reception area. He complied and then, with a vacant look, slumped down on the sofa. I cautiously picked the gun up by its barrel and took it to my secretary's desk and asked her to wrap it in a cloth and lock it in a drawer until the police took it. Then I asked Dan Brooks, a young partner, who also had come out of his office, to call the police while I made some calls to get an ambulance immediately. It was not long before the police and ambulance drivers arrived. I then had the horrible experience of watching my classmate, strapped to a gurney, being wheeled out of our offices, reasonably certain that he was dead.

Al's former student, Dennis Sweeney, sat despondent on the sofa saying not a word until the police finished marking the outline of where Al's body had been found and finally placing him under arrest. I did recall hearing him tell one of the officers that he had heard voices through the fillings in his teeth, saying that Al had become an evil force whom he should eliminate. Two officers led him out of the office. Our staff was traumatized and frightened. I told them to go home and, as it was Friday, to try to recover over the weekend. I stayed in the office, stunned, unable to do anything.

At about 9:30 that night, the phone rang and someone in my office who was still there picked it up and buzzed me to say it was a Mr. Steven Smith from the Kennedy campaign who wished to speak to me. I picked up the phone.

"Mr. Layton," he said. "This is Steve Smith from the Kennedy campaign. We would like you to make certain that neither you or any of your staff, in responding to media inquiries, make any reference to Al's having any connection with or having done any work for the Kennedy campaign. We wish to keep our name out of this mess."

I was furious and burst out, "Why you supercilious son of a bitch! My classmate has just been gun downed in my offices and you're only concerned with keeping the Kennedy name out of this, although he spent the last three months of his life working for you! Well, I'll do exactly as I please without taking any instruction from you!"

With that, I slammed the phone down. What a world full of phonies Al was connected with!

Al's volunteer secretary quietly packed her things along with all Al's files and moved out. She appeared somewhat crushed by the whole series of weird events, as were many of us.

Only several hours after his body had been removed did I happen to remember the $1000 that I had told him to keep and that he had placed back in his pants pocket. I asked one of the young lawyers who had stayed on that day to call the hospital to find out if they found the money and, of course, they said none was found on him. In later conversations with colleagues, I discovered to my surprise as a life long New Yorker that this was a common occurrence under the circumstances.

The following day, I drove up to my weekend house in Lakeville, spent time chopping wood and trying to recover from this incident. Normally, chopping wood was a task I left to others, but that day I had so much pent-up anger that I found it a necessary release.

The only person that I ever heard from regarding Al was his ex-wife, who lived in Boston with their young son. She was in New York to attend Sweeney's sentencing, where he was given an indeterminate sentence to a psychiatric facility. She asked if I could meet her because she had a problem she wanted to discuss. I invited her for lunch and discovered that she was a lovely person. Her concern was her young son, who was having terrible nightmares thinking that the man who killed his father might be planning to kill him as well. I was sympathetic and suggested that consulting a child psychiatrist in Boston might be worthwhile. Secondly, I suggested that she call the New York County DA's office and ask them to notify her by mail in advance of any bail or release application made by Sweeney so she could appear in court to oppose it; otherwise, it might be possible for him to be released after a short number of years. I reminded the DA's office of her request whenever possible. I do know that on several occasions she successfully opposed Sweeney's efforts to be released as she would phone me when she was in town.

Dennis Sweeney was released from any level of custody in 2000.

30

How I Bested the New York Times

While working at the Office of Legal Counsel in the Department of Justice in the late 50s, I had been occasionally sent over to the Japanese Embassy to discuss disputed treaty language issues with their Legal Attaché, a certain Mr. Tetsuo Sato. He and I got along extremely well and it is fair to say that over the year or two that we worked with each other, we became very good friends. While it is not customary in Japan to bring business acquaintances to one's home, he invited me to visit his apartment to meet his wife and two small boys for a Sunday American-style brunch. On that occasion, he also asked that I call him 'Tet' and he called me 'Bob'.

We got along so well, in fact, that when each of us planned to leave government service, we began discussing how we could keep our business connection open through our private law firms in our respective countries. We planned to refer clients each to the other on international legal matters and later try to form an international firm. No clients immediately sought us out and for several years we were mostly Christmas card exchangers between New York and Tokyo.

I then learned from Tet that his return to the Tokyo law firm, which had been called Blakemore & Sato, after three years in the United States, had not been a happy one. Japanese custom regarding seniority prevented regaining his former position as the senior Japanese lawyer in the firm, which was headed by a prominent American lawyer, Mr. Thomas Blakemore. His position had not only been taken by the next senior Japanese lawyer, but his name was removed from the name of the firm.

The replacement, Mr. Matsuki, was an indifferent lawyer with little imagination and no serious international experience. He was also petty, arrogant and determined to lord himself over Tet. Unable to bear a humiliating experience professionally as well as personally, Tet had decided to leave the firm to open his own office together with an older Japanese lawyer, a Mr. Tsuda, who was planning to retire from his career as a government attorney. Tet's father had been, at one time, the Attorney General of Japan. He believed that, in the Japanese culture, this would aid in the development of his practice.

Coincidentally, I had just been retained by a large U.S. defense contractor and was planning, as well, to start my own firm.

I asked if he had discussed this situation with Mr.

Blakemore and was told that he had. He said that Blakemore very much regretted the situation but was powerless to reverse their positions even though he acknowledged that Matsuki was not a very capable lawyer. But Blakemore promised that he would see to Sato's success in his new practice by referring every client conflict situation he encountered to Tet's new firm. Since Blakemore already represented many large U.S. corporations that did business in Japan, conflicts continually arose when U.S. competitors of his clients sought to retain him.

This development presented the first opportunity for us to work together for he now could make referrals to me in New York and I expressed my delight at the prospect of our working together once again. My early success at attracting clients was satisfying, but none of that work was international in nature, and I felt that referrals from Tet Sato would be more interesting. Tom Blakemore turned out to be as good as his word. Sato's new practice blossomed.

On his first visit to New York, after opening his office, he asked me to help him with an assignment he was taking on for Nissan Corporation, the maker of Datsun motor vehicles. Nissan planned to purchase a General Motors plant located outside of Lima, Peru, and the contract with

GM was expected to contain a guarantee under New York law, which it would be my task to deal with. Thus began one of the longest business/personal relationships of my legal career, and one which contributed much pleasure as well as financial success to me and later, to my family.

The actual call regarding the GM plant in Peru came shortly thereafter when Tet asked me to join the Nissan 19-person negotiating team at a hotel outside Lima. He said he would be flying over two or three days later, as he was enmeshed in an emergency negotiation in Tokyo. However, he did not arrive until some 12 days later and I was forced to take his place in the negotiations, well outside the subject of the New York guarantee. Fortunately, my English came in handy in speaking with the GM attorneys who used me as a conduit to the Japanese executives when deadlock was reached on some subjects. It was a strenuous period. I was awakened at 7 a.m. each morning by the youngest members of the Nissan team, accompanied to breakfast, and driven to pick up our local Peruvian counsel, and thence, to the GM plant, where lengthy, formal discussions took place all day. In the evening, back in our hotel rooms, we had to write lengthy telexes in longhand to senior management in Tokyo, reporting each clause that had been agreed to during the day, the open issues, the compromises on the table and asking for instructions for the following day's meetings.

Tet Sato's arrival was delayed until the middle of the night prior to the final day of the negotiations, and I was hauled out of bed at 2 a.m. in order to comply with Japanese protocol and greet my friend as he alighted from the airplane at the Lima airport.

Over the years, through him I represented the Japan Tobacco and Salt Corporation (that country's tobacco monopoly) both in New York City and in contract negotiations in various parts of the United States. In addition, I became the U.S. counsel for the Nomura Trading Corporation, an importer and distributor of large, computerized commercial sewing machines throughout all parts of the United States. I also negotiated some transactions for *The Yomiuri Shimbun*, the second-largest newspaper in Japan. All of this interesting international legal work came to me as a result of my relationship with 'Satosan', a name that Tet used for his telex address as well as his nickname. I followed with 'Laytosan' for my firm's telex address. Our relationship became extremely close on a personal as well as a business basis, with visits to each other's homes as well as offices.

All of which leads up to one of the strangest assignments I had ever been asked to undertake. In early

1982, Satosan phoned me on behalf of the extremely wealthy and established family that owned *The Yomiuri Shimbun*. In the Tokyo edition of *The New York Times*, a front page article, below a large, top right-hand corner headline, by Richard Halloran, its Tokyo Bureau Chief, reported that the patriarch of the family, who had died several years earlier, had been on the payroll of the chief counter-spy agency of the United States, the OSS, during, as well as after World War II. Such an accusation of disloyalty to his country blackened his reputation and that of the family. It was for that reason that I was being retained to commence a lawsuit for many millions of dollars against the *Times* unless a complete retraction was promptly made. I had to tell Satosan that, according to New York law, the right of an individual to sue for damages did not survive his death. In other words, those rights did not pass on to his heirs, and therefore no lawsuit would survive a routine motion to dismiss it. He replied that the family would not care; that they wanted vengeance for such outrageous besmirching of his good name and the patently libelous conduct. I could only reply that I would do my best, that I had a friend on the legal staff of the *Times* and would start work immediately. But I cautioned him to tell the family not to get their hopes too high.

I did call that friend on the *Times* in-house legal staff, who was an expert on libel/defamation law, and he confirmed my belief that no suit was permissible. He did tell me that Abe Rosenthal, the Managing Editor, had a strict requirement that any significant factual statement in a *Times* news story was required to have two independently verifiable sources, in order to protect against just such claims as the ones my clients were making. He would speak to Mr. Rosenthal about the matter and verify that the two sources did exist. I thanked him and still went to work on a possible complaint.

The following day, I got a call back. Mr. Rosenthal had assured my friend that the two sources did exist, and that no retraction would be forthcoming. I was miffed and suspicious regarding the two alleged, independent sources but there was not very much I could do. I thought it foolish to bring a lawsuit which, on strict, legal theory grounds, would be dismissed, whatever the truth or untruth of the alleged spying activities of the family patriarch. I had a largely sleepless night until I remembered a grammar school friend from Queens who had also become a lawyer, who had very good Kennedy administration connections. The remembrance was critical because I knew that he had become General Counsel of the CIA, the successor to the wartime OSS.

Early the following morning, I phoned him at his home in Cleveland Heights, a Washington suburb where I had spent several weekends with his family when making business trips to D.C. After describing the situation in some detail, I asked if it was possible to have the OSS records examined quietly to see if the family patriarch's name appeared there. My friend told me that he would think it over and call me back in a couple of days. He did, and told me then that he would have it looked at, but that our conversation was strictly off the record. I readily agreed. Two days later he called to say that he had the information that I was interested in but that the only way I could get it was by flying to Washington, spending the weekend at his house as his family's guest, and that during my stay he and I would take a long walk in the woods, at which time I would learn the information that had been found, and that nothing would be in writing.

I flew down and had that walk in the woods. There, he told me that there was not a scintilla of evidence that the gentleman in question had been in the employ of 'the Agency' as the phrase was often used. Not only had not a dollar—or a yen—been paid to him, but neither did his name appear anywhere in the files. I repeated the claim made in the *Times* article, which he had read, but emphasized the Abe Rosenthal two-independent-source-verification tale, to which he simply chuckled.

"It's your pleasure to deal with Mr. Rosenthal, not mine, but I know that what I've told you is fact."

He made me promise that his name would never be used as a source for the information I now had, and we finished our walk on the understanding that this subject between us was now closed—forever.

On returning to New York, I phoned my friend at the *Times* to tell him, in a guarded fashion, that I had discovered from unimpeachable sources in Washington that there wasn't a speck of truth in Mr. Halloran's story and asked once more that a retraction be published. He said that he would speak to Rosenthal again and call me. He did that later in the same afternoon telling me that Rosenthal said that the story stands and that I could sue or do whatever else I cared to but as far as *The New York Times* was concerned, the case was closed. I was furious and, uncharacteristically, I believe, just spewed up something I made up out of whole cloth:

"Just tell your Mr. Rosenthal and his venerable publisher Mr. Sulzberger, that they better not be planning any trips to Japan in the near future because—while here, the law is against us—in Japan what they have done is a *crime* and their asses are going to be dragged off an airplane and into a prison if they ever do come there."

My friend at the *Times* just said, "Calm down, Bob. You've tried your best, now let's forget the whole thing."

I hung up and called for my secretary to prepare and send a final bill to the client. In my covering letter to Tet and the family, I strongly recommended that no suit be filed and they should try to put the matter into the past. The legal time came to a bill for $2500. I took the bill down the hall to show it to my young partner who knew all about the case. I told him about the final kiss-off from the *Times,* but I left out my outburst and we then went back to our more routine activities.

A week passed when I received a frantic call from my legal friend at the *Times*.

"Bob, you've got to help me. Please have your clients call the police at Narita Airport to make sure that Mr. Rosenthal and Mr. Sulzberger are not arrested. Their plane should be landing in two hours from now!"

"Why in the world would I want to do that, considering what they have done?" I replied.

"Because the *Times* printed a full retraction on the first page of the second section of today's paper. The people in

Tokyo should've had it twelve hours ago so they can verify it, and I sent a copy over to you by messenger a half hour ago. You should be getting it any minute now. I never thought those two would decide to make a business trip without telling me in advance. I just found out last night."

I thanked him, and sure enough the messenger arrived and the retraction was as complete and full as we could've wanted. I went down the hall again to show the *Times* retraction to my young partner who shouted:

"Get that stupid $2500 bill back! You did a *Clark Clifford* $25,000 job, not a measly $2500 insult to us! I'm serious, Layton. Just send a telex explaining that there was a typo in the bill that we just caught. They'll understand and will pay it. They must be happy as hell."

"I can't do that," I countered. "That is the bill I sent and it was a week ago. Even if the client were inclined to pay it, Tet Sato has followed this very closely and I could not look him in the eye again if I tried to do something like you suggest. But I am sorry those birds didn't plan that trip much earlier."

And so ended my triumph over *The New York Times.* I'm not sure if they ever found out what the criminal law of Japan provided under the circumstances. I know that I never looked it up.

31

A Leopard Doesn't Change Its Spots

Early 1974 brought with it an unpleasant event in my legal career. Based upon an early decision of my firm that we would do pro bono work up to 20% of our time with the same legal effort and care that we expended for our regular clients, we had agreed to assist a number of young lawyers from Buffalo, New York. They were representing the inmates at Attica Prison who had been brutalized by prison guards and militiamen sent in to quell the riots at the direction of then Governor Nelsen A. Rockefeller. The Buffalo lawyers had brought a lawsuit with Rockefeller as its principal defendant in the Federal District Court for the Southern District of New York, our local Federal courthouse. All these lawyers asked us for was a place to work, the use of our library, and our advice and local counsel type of assistance.

One evening they knocked on my door with a question. Their question to me was due to their just having learned that their suit against Rockefeller, et. al., had been assigned to Judge Harold Tyler; they knew that Rockefeller's lawyers were planning to file a motion to move the case to the Federal court in Buffalo, a venue much friendlier to

Governor Rockefeller. They wanted me to tell them what Tyler was likely to do in such a scenario. I said that I would phone Tyler to give me an idea of how the change of venue motion might best be handled. When he heard my question about the change of venue motion, he said:

"Tell them not to worry about it. I rarely grant them. After they are served they should send a short note to my Calendar Clerk stating that they oppose the motion. And the rest will follow in regular course."

Although this seemed extremely informal and irregular, I reported it to the Buffalo lawyers and they then followed the instructions. They were in the courtroom when one of Tyler's clerks handed out copies of a 15-page Opinion, treating the young lawyers' informal note to his Calendar Clerk as their answer to the motion, and rattling on at length with reasons why the case deserved to be transferred to Buffalo, many copied word for word from the Rockefeller lawyers' papers. In other words, Tyler had used me to trick the Buffalo lawyers.

The following morning's *New York Times* featured a picture of Nelson Rockefeller being sworn in as Vice-President of the United States by new President Gerald Ford, and a few days later a short announcement that Ford had nominated Tyler to be Deputy Attorney General along with Rudolph Giuliani, his most recent favorite sidekick, as Assistant Deputy Attorney General. Being a cynic, I had no doubt that Tyler had already been wooing Rockefeller for support in his new effort for a high post in Washington. I, and my innocent Buffalo advisees were quickly sacrificed; the Federal judge in Buffalo protected Rockefeller, and I was ignored in much the same way as I had been when he left me high and dry in 1961 after promising to teach me how to try civil jury cases. I also had suspicions about how the Attica riot cases had been assigned to Tyler in the first place.

I did get one brief piece of revenge in late 1987 after returning from some ten horrible weeks heading the Jordache /Nakash legal team in Los Angeles where we were battling the Guess/Marciano forces on behalf of the Jones Day law firm. It had acquired the entire Surrey & Morse firm. After the merger, I was appointed as head of the New York Office Litigation Department. Now, I was asked to take the depositions of three important witnesses at the Jones Day offices in Manhattan.

I had the witnesses served and awaited the outcry. It came from Tyler's new law firm, Patterson Belknap, which he had joined after Ford lost to Carter and he had returned to New York. A motion to stop the depositions was signed by Tyler and brought before one of his former colleagues, a District Judge whose chambers adjoined those of Tyler before he had departed for D.C. again. Tyler thought that surely his old judicial colleague would take care of him. But he did not reckon with the fact that by that time I had appeared before his former colleague many times and had earned his respect. The motion was heard on a cold November day, and as I hung up my hat and coat in the anteroom, I heard Tyler saying loudly to his crew of lawyers:

"Well, look who's here today, sporting such a fancy chapeau! None other than my friend, Mr. Layton!"

I took my seat at the counsel table, and turned back to whisper to him: "I wonder if you'll be as chipper when your argument to stop these depositions is denied." Silence ensued.

His former colleague took the bench, welcomed Tyler warmly, and asked him why my deposition notices were not proper. Thus, began a bad day for former judge Tyler. He began by stumbling around with the facts, which he was obviously not familiar with; it got worse when he directed himself to legal arguments, which had always been his weakness. Amazingly, he begged off by suggesting that one of his associates was more familiar with "the file" than he was, as though knowing about the case that he was arguing was unimportant for a man of his stature. This got nowhere with the judge, who said:

"Thank you, Judge Tyler. I think I'll hear from Mr. Layton right now."

I stood and said, "I think Your Honor will find all the controlling authorities set out in our brief; none of the considerations thrown around in Judge Tyler's papers are relevant in our circumstances. I suggest we discuss some dates for the depositions."

The Judge agreed and Tyler was heard from again only when he said that none of the proposed dates were convenient for him. The Judge said that he understood and asked that one of the accompanying Patterson Belknap lawyers cover the depositions, and dates were quickly agreed to. The Judge thanked us all and left. I beat it out of that courtroom as fast as I could, conspicuously quipping to Tyler, largely with tongue in cheek: "Sorry I won't be seeing you at the depositions."

That incident effectively ended my legal involvements with the great "Ace" Tyler, a most disappointing man, if there ever was one. He died, I discovered, some years later, in the Township of Salisbury, of which Lakeville, my present home is a part, but I never spoke to him again.

Epilogue

As I am bringing closure to this Memoir, I recall that some 50 years after we each left Flushing High School to go off to different colleges, Don Holden and I were brought together again at the conclusion of our respective careers. He had been in publishing, was a museum director, and a successful artist. I had a most satisfying and successful career as an international litigator.

A mutual friend of ours from our boyhood days bumped into Don at a museum in Washington, D.C. and gave him my telephone number in Manhattan, suggesting that he call me as I "had not turned out badly over the years." I received Don's call, we chatted happily, at the close of which he insisted that I join him for tea on the following Thursday at his most favorite place, The Century Association, on West 43rd Street. We met there at 4 p.m. and hugged each other immediately. After exchanging many details concerning our present lives, children, wives, etc., Don stated that he was going to sponsor me for membership in The Century. I told him that I already belonged to the Yale Club and didn't need a second club, but he insisted, and due to his persistence and thanks to the pro bono work I had done for art and music organizations over the years, I did become a member after a few years.

Shortly thereafter, I was in New York one day for a scheduled lunch, which got cancelled at the last minute, and finding myself with no one to lunch with, decided to try the advice that I had been given to come, when alone, to eat at the Long Table on the third floor of the Club for a pleasant experience. Only the week before, I had been recommended by my longtime friend Donald Landsman, to read a new memoir written by a New Yorker editor named Gardner Botsford. I did so and enjoyed it greatly. On arriving at the Long Table, I saw an elderly gentleman sitting there alone. Walking over to him, I said, "Hello. How are you?"

He said, "Lonely."

"No longer," said I, and sat down next to him, saying, "My name is Bob Layton."

"My name is Gardner Botsford," he replied.

That introduction began a wonderful lunch as I told him how much I enjoyed reading his book. We were soon joined by members from *Time* as well as *Newsweek* for an extended lunch. Each of them knew Gardner and were then introduced to me.

*   *   *   *

The end of my active law practice motivated me to write this memoir, which has given me great pleasure. I now await the next, and perhaps last, chapter of my life.

Acknowledgments

I could not have written this Memoir without the support and advice of my lovely wife Christine, who has been unendingly supportive at every difficult step, since this is the first, and perhaps, last book that I have taken the trouble to write. She has also served as an editor of the final text, along with my good friend Dick Grossman.

My two daughters, Elisabeth and Julie, have been willing contributors of ideas and suggestions from their generational point of view. I trust that I will be able to make up for the time I took away from being with them during this effort.

The Scoville Memorial Library in Salisbury, Connecticut and its Director Claudia Cayne, gave birth to this memoir by sponsoring a Memoir Writing Class, led by Carol Ascher, to whom I will be forever grateful. She further spent much time with me on a one-on-one basis after I left her course.

I would be ungrateful if I did not add my friend Robert Kipniss, the artist and author, to whom I sent many individual chapters, for his insightful comments as well as encouragement. Also, my thanks go to my friend and neighbor Rick Knight, whose outstanding computer skills assisted me immensely in completing my manuscript.

—Bob Layton

Lakeville, CT

Recommended Reading

Wilkey, Malcolm, *As the Twig Is Bent*,
USA: Xlibiris Corporation, 2003

Thomas, Evan, *Ike's Bluff*, New York: Little, Brown and
Company, 2012

Ambrose, Stephen E., *Eisenhower, Soldier and President,*
New York: Simon & Schuster, 1990

Heymann, David, *RFK: A Candid Biography of Robert F.
Kennedy,* Dutton Adult, 1998

Reeves, Richard, *President Kennedy, Profile of Power,*
New York, Simon & Schuster, 1993

Made in the USA
San Bernardino, CA
13 August 2013